Hooked on Science!

Hooked on Science!

READY-TO-USE DISCOVERY ACTIVITIES FOR GRADES 4–8

Susan Breyer Sewall

THE CENTER FOR APPLIED
RESEARCH IN EDUCATION
West Nyack, New York 10995

© 1990 by

THE CENTER FOR APPLIED
RESEARCH IN EDUCATION

West Nyack, New York

All rights reserved.

10   9   8   7   6   5   4   3

Library of Congress Cataloging-in-Publication Data

Sewall, Susan Breyer, 1984–
    Hooked on science! : ready-to-use discovery activities for grades
4-8 / Susan Breyer Sewall.
      p.   cm.
    Includes bibliographical references.
    ISBN 0-87628-404-7
    1. Natural history—Study and teaching (Elementary) 2. Nature
study. I. Title.
QH51.S48 1990   89-25239
372.3′57044—dc20   CIP

ISBN 0-87628-404-7

**THE CENTER FOR APPLIED
RESEARCH IN EDUCATION
BUSINESS & PROFESSIONAL DIVISION**
A division of Simon & Schuster
West Nyack, New York 10995

Printed in the United States of America

FOR
MY VERSION OF THE THREE WISE MEN:

Dr. John Rosengren
The person who let me discover that science is great fun.

Dr. Matthew J. Brennan
The person who showed me how to really see our world.

Jim Melody
Superintendent of Delaware Valley Schools
The person who encourages me, no matter how crazy the idea!

Acknowledgements

Many thanks to the people who have helped, supported and
guided me as this book evolved:
Peggy, Catie and Jeffrey, my children, who patiently
encouraged me.
My friends Scott Palermo and Cindy Piatt, who spent many
hours proofreading this manuscript and suggested ways to
make it better.

About the Author

Susan Breyer Sewall has over seventeen years of classroom teaching experience and has written and presented extensively on how to set up environmental education programs and how to use children's literature to teach science. Her awards include a Gustav Ohaus/National Science Teachers Association Award in 1984 and Pennsylvania Alliance for Environmental Education's Outstanding Environmental Teacher of the Year award in 1987.

Ms. Sewall has a Master's degree in Environmental Studies from Montclair State College in Upper Montclair, New Jersey, and a B.A. in Elementary Education from William Paterson College in Wayne, New Jersey.

About This Resource

Hooked On Science! provides a store of exciting, easy-to-use activities to enrich and reinforce all areas of the general science curriculum in grades 4 through 8. Each activity includes complete teacher instructions, worksheets, or handouts as needed, and suggestions for extension activities. Also included are instructions for making or obtaining inexpensive supplies and equipment, frequently using recycled materials.

For your teaching convenience, *Hooked on Science* is organized into six units:

1. **Critters and Creatures**. A variety of activities that focus on insects, spiders, earthsworms, birds, endangered species, and the food web.
2. **Wonders of the Green World**. Students learn about unusual uses for common plants, including how to make violet jelly; the unit focuses on the tree's role in the environment, and more.
3. **Outdoor Activities & Equipment**. Students invent tracks and try to elude capture, study wind with "quick kites," perform a water quality survey using equipment made from recycled materials, and identify patterns found in nature.
4. **Thinking Like Scientists**. Here is a full array of activities to encourage students' use of the scientific method, including two ideal September projects, "Time Capsule" and "Seating Chart Sleuthing."
5. **Recycling**. Activities demonstrate how we can recycle and how nature already recycles, culminating in a "Recycled Invention Convention."
6. **What Else?** This unit includes a special activity for a snowy day, a natural history book project—written by students, science board games for reviews and putting together "A Week with a Theme."

With the high-interest activities in this book, it's easy to tap into the natural curiosity students have about their world and how it works. And when students are allowed to discover science through hands-on experiences, science class isn't just work—it's fun! Students learn with more efficiency and deeper understanding because the topics are part of their world. They learn to conduct research because it's essential to finding the answer to a question important to them. They learn to connect at first seemingly unrelated ideas into plausible explanations. Creative problem solving is natural when students are attempting to find answers that matter.

If you are planning a year's worth of supplemental activities, it would be a good idea to skim through the book, reading the short overviews which accompany each activity. The Table of Contents will also help. Feel free to adapt these activities to fit your own needs, and remember that wonder and excitement are a big part of what science is all about!

Susan Breyer Sewall

Table of Contents

Hooked on Science!

CRITTERS AND CREATURES

THE INCREDIBLE INSECT EXHIBIT

INTRODUCTION

When the course of study requires that the class study insects, looking at both the harmful and helpful ones, this activity makes the study come alive. The students prepare a display and everyone votes for the best in each category.

OVERVIEW

Each member of the class researches a specific insect and then prepares an exhibit about that insect. The entry must include a series of drawings that illustrate the stages of the insect's life, food sources, predators, and details of behaviors which make that insect unique.

Students create a desk top display as their entry in the "Incredible Insect Exhibit." They arrange their displays, and the whole class tours the exhibit area. Each student briefly explains his/her exhibit as the class comes to it.

When all of the exhibits have been presented, each member of the class votes by secret ballot for the winners of each category.

PROCEDURE

1. Decide which insects are appropriate for the students to research. A list of suggestions is included as potential study possibilities. If you want, duplicate the list, and cut out the names on the list to make individual slips of paper. Or, write the names of the insects on slips of paper and fold them.

2. Place the slips in a gift-wrapped box. (As you walk to the front of the room, all eyes will be on you!)

3. Announce the beginning of the "Incredible Insect Exhibit." Students will select, at random, one insect and prepare an exhibit about it. The exhibit must include:

   —three or four drawings of the insect as it progresses through its life stages (egg–larva–pupa–adult OR egg–nymphs–adult).

   —The adult drawing must label the head, thorax and abdomen of the insect.

—Students must discover what the insect eats throughout its life and what preys on the insect.

—The exhibit also needs to include information about the insect's habitat and any other details that make it unusual.

—Students may include any other materials that they wish, as long as everything fits on the top of one desk.

4. Open the wrapped box, and allow each member of the class to select one of the slips of paper. After each student has selected a slip of paper from the box, any student who is unhappy with his/her selection may return the slip to the box and pick another. Switching and swapping is allowed, as long as both parties are agreeable.

5. Students research their insects, and prepare their exhibits. To make the displays stand up, see MAKING THE FRAME instructions at the end of this activity.

Students should be finished in about one week of class time. As always, circulate among the students as they work to make sure that any questions are answered, encouragement is given and they are on task.

If the class is unfamiliar with research technique, duplicate the INCREDIBLE INSECT EXHIBIT RESEARCH SHEET at the end of this activity, and allow the students to use the form as a guide for the research of their insects.

6. A few days before the exhibits are due, discuss the categories for which awards will be given. After listing the possible categories, ask the class to suggest other categories for possible awards. If the students can provide good reasons for a category, by all means include it!

By discussing the categories a few days prior to the actual presentations, the teacher has ample time to prepare ribbons and certificates. Make sure that there are enough ribbons and certificates for each student to receive one.

Possible Categories

Best Looking

Best Tricks for Survival

Most Likely to Succeed

Weirdest Lifestyle

Most Economic Damage

Best Use of Color for Camouflage Purposes

Best Symbiosis Team
Most Misunderstood by People

Good Friend of the Earth

Most Ingenious Locomotion

Best Friend to People

Worst Enemy of People

Funniest-Looking

Wildest Coloring

Most Impressive Defense

Most Offensive Smell

Most Effective World-Wide Distribution

Hang a large poster on a bulletin board with all of the categories listed—to remind the class of the areas in which the insects can be named as winners.

7. On the big day, allow the students five minutes to set up the displays. Then, as a class, move from display to display, with each student pointing out what the insect looks like, what eats it and what it eats, as well as any unusual characteristics. The student should suggest a specific judging category for the entry.

8. When all of the displays have been presented, give the students ballots, and allow them to silently vote for the ones they feel are best in each category. The completed ballot should be put in a sealed box. Once the ballot is in the box, it can only be removed for counting. (See JUDGING THE INCREDIBLE INSECT EXHIBIT ballot at the end of this activity.)

9. Tabulate the results, announce which entries were voted to which categories. Present awards to each student within each category. The awards can be a ribbon, (See WATER CLEARING DEVICES) a certificate, or some other method of recognition. Each student should receive an award.

10. Discuss the project with the class.

   —Point out that insects are a very successful group of living things, and ask the class to give reasons why insects are such successful creatures.

   —Ask the students to explain how some insects are helpful to people and other creatures.

   —Students should also discuss pesticides, why they are used, what effects the pesticides have on the targeted insects and what the side-effects of pesticides are.

EXTENSIONS

1. This activity might be done for a parent "Open House." The students can be available to discuss the merits of their insects with the guests.

2. This can be done with almost any type of plant, animal or whatever. Just change the exhibit requirements, the categories and whatever else is appropriate, and go for it!

3. If you have a group of kids who are really into this, have them dress up as their insects as they present them!

RESOURCES

Headstrom, Richard. *Adventures With Insects*. New York: Dover Publications, Inc., 1982.

> Information about insects written as a dialogue. The diagrams along the margins give the book a journal-like quality.

Selsam, Millicent E. and Ronald Goor. *Backyard Insects*. New York: Scholastic Book Services, 1981.

> Wonderful photos and lively text about the most common insects.

Selsam, Millicent E. *Where Do They Go? Insects in Winter.* New York: Scholastic Book Services, 1981.

> Answers to the question in the title. For the younger students who are undertaking this project.

Zim, Herbert and Cottam, Clarence. *Insects*. New York: Golden Press, 1963.

> The easy-to-read text gives the student much of the information that he/she needs to begin the research phase of this project.

━━ ALL SORTS OF INSECTS FOR THE CLASS TO STUDY ━━

INCOMPLETE METAMORPHOSIS:

Insects that have three stages: (egg–nymph–adult)

annual cicada	field cricket	red-banded leafhopper
American cockroach	green darner	shieldbug
American grasshopper	green stinkbug	short-nosed cattle louse
aphids	harlequin bug	spittlebug
blackwing damselfly	katydid mole cricket	squashbug
Buffalo treehopper	lateral leafhopper	stonefly
camel cricket	lubber grasshopper	termite
Carolina grasshopper	mayfly	terrapin scale
Carolina mantis	milkweed bug	3-banded leafhopper
cinch bug	mormon cricket	walking stick
dragonfly	periodical cicada	
earwig	praying mantis	

COMPLETE METAMORPHOSIS:

Insects that have four stages: (egg - larva - pupa - adult)

American burying beetle	dog flea	polyphemus moth
ant lion	firefly	potter wasp
bald-faced hornet	fruit fly	promethea moth
banded woollybear moth	giant swallowtail butterfly	rove beetle
brown lacewing	golden-eye lacewing	scarab beetle
caddisfly	gypsy moth	scorpionfly
carpenter ants	horse fly	sphinx moths
carpet beetle	Japanese beetle	striped blister beetle
carrion beetle	June beetle	tachid fly
cecropia moth	ladybird beetle	tent caterpillar
click beetle	leaf-cutting bee	tiger beetles
cotton boll weevil	luna moth	tiger swallowtail butterfly
crane fly	monarch butterfly	twelve-spotted cucumber beetle
diving beetle	mosquito	unicorn beetle
deer fly	mud dauber wasp	viceroy butterfly
dobson fly	pine sawyer	

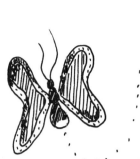

INCREDIBLE INSECT EXHIBIT RESEARCH SHEET

1. The name of my insect is_____.

2. It has _____ stages in its life. (three or four)
   If it goes through three stages, its stages are **egg - nymph - adult**. The nymphs look like little adults! If if goes through four stages, its stages are **egg - larva - pupa - adult**. In each of the stages, the insects always look different.

3. My insect eats:_____.

4. It catches its food by: _____

   _____

5. It is food for: _____.

6. People think that my insect: _____

   _____

(Things that might fit in here are: my insect causes harm to plants and/or other living things, it doesn't bother anything, it helps the world because it eats other insects, or it harms things that people don't care about.)

7. My insect lays its eggs on: _____

   _____.

8. Find drawings or pictures of your insect in all of its stages. Draw each stage on a separate piece of paper for the display. Make sure that you label the insect's head, thorax, and abdomen in the adult picture.

9. Are there any unusual habits that your insect has?

   _____

   _____.

10. For what judging categories do you think your insect qualifies?

   _____

   _____.

Name_____   Date_____

JUDGING THE INCREDIBLE INSECT EXHIBIT

Write the name of the insect you believe should win in each of the following categories:

Best Looking

_____

Good Friend of the Earth

_____

Best Tricks for Survival

_____

Most Ingenious Locomotion

_____

Most Likely to Succeed

_____

Best Use of Color

_____

Best Symbiosis Team

_____

Most Misunderstood by People

_____

Most Effective

_____

Best Friend to People

_____

Weirdest Lifestyle

_____

Worst Enemy of People

_____

Most Economic Damage

_____

Funniest Looking

_____

Wildest Looking

_____

Most Impressive Defense

_____

Most Offensive Smell

_____

MAKING THE FRAME

When the students prepare their Incredible Insect Exhibits, they need to prepare a means by which the drawings can stand up. There are several possibilities.

The styrofoam meat tray method

1. Wash a styrofoam meat tray with soap and water. Cut the tray as indicated.
2. Bend back the cutout section. It will snap and break. Put the piece in the position desired, and tape it with clear tape.
3. Glue or tape the insect illustrations onto the trays, and allow to dry.

   If styrofoam meat trays are not available, recycled cardboard, clear plastic meat trays, clear fast food salad containers or any other hard material will do.

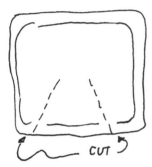

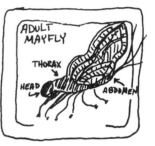

Zig-zag method

Students can also tape together their cards so they zig-zag forward and backward.

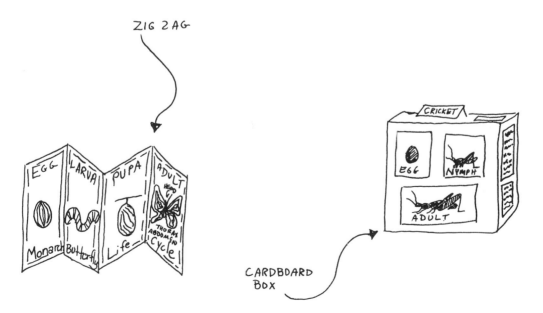

Large cardboard box method

Have the students prepare their exhibits on a large box (but it still must fit on the desk). The pictures can be taped or pasted on the side of the box, the other information can be on the top of the box.

ENDANGERED AND EXTINCT

INTRODUCTION

Plants and animals become extinct for many reasons. Changes in habitat, food supplies, and adaptations of other sorts all take a toll in species extinction. People have had a serious effect on the number of species that have become extinct. Although extinctions have occurred since the world began, human actions have increased the rate at which species disappear. This series of activities focuses on why various animals become extinct.

It is important to remember that the gloom and doom approach to this activity is to be avoided at all costs. The activity should be enlightening, not devastating.

ENDANGERED SPECIES POSTER SERIES

OVERVIEW

Students research endangered plants and animals, then create an informative poster explaining the reasons why that species is endangered.

PROCEDURE

1. Ask the students if they can name any plants or animals that are extinct. List the correct replies on the board.
2. When students have listed as many extinct animals and plants as they can think of, ask if anyone in the class can explain why one of the animals/plants listed became extinct.

3. Explain that the class is going to prepare a poster series on animals and plants which are *near extinction*—Endangered Species.

4. Have the class suggest reasons why animals become endangered or extinct. When completed, the list should include: loss of habitat, loss of defenses through genetic adaptation, climate change, food supply change, habitat change, or any other reasonable suggestion.

5. Ask each member of the class to research one plant or animal on the endangered list that you provide for them. (No list is provided here because that list changes. For a list, see a current almanac.)

Each student will be asked to:

      —draw a picture of his/her animal/plant

      —describe its habitat, what it eats, and what eats it

      —explain why that plant/animal is on the endangered list

6. After allowing the class time to research and prepare their posters, ask each student to explain their poster to the class. Hang the posters on a bulletin board or in a hallway.

REALLY EXTINCT!

OVERVIEW

Since the class has prepared the poster series, and they should have the basics of why animals and plants become extinct, why not allow them to use some creative talent and invent their own animals and plants? But no calm posters this time. The students must dress up as the creature that they create...and explain why they have become extinct.

PROCEDURE

1. Have the class review reasons for extinction.
2. Announce that sometimes it is good to think beyond conventional thought and be creative. Now is one of those times. Tell the class that they are going to make up their own extinct plant or animal and dress up like whatever it is they create.
3. Each student will need to include the following in his or her oral report:

    —the name of the creature

    —what habitat it lived in

    —what was its prey

    —what were its predators

    —how did the animal or plant defend itself

    —what its den, nest, cave, or shelter was like

    —why it became extinct

If the students are stuck in a conventional mode, create an outlandish creature as an example. (See REALLY EXTINCT instruction sheet.)

4. Encourage the students to use recycled materials whenever possible. It is important for students to learn to reuse materials whenever possible.
5. Students may seek advice from parents, friends, or anyone else who will help to make the project fun and creative, but most of the actual work should be done by the student.
6. On the day of the presentations, make sure there is room in the classroom for the storage of costumes and equipment.

EXTENSIONS

1. You might want to photograph all of the creatures. Ask the class to try to develop a classification system for the strange creatures!

Name _____   Date _____

REALLY EXTINCT

When you create YOUR creature...
please be sure to include the following:

* the creature's name
* the habitat of the creature
* what it ate
* what ate it
* how did it defend itself?
* what was its cave, den, nest or shelter like?
* why did it become extinct?

Make sure that you use recycled materials!

Webbed-footed alligator tooth cleaner.

This project is due on _____

2. Ask a local game warden to come to talk to the class about the local endangered plants and animals.

3. Using an almanac, find out which animals are currently on the top ten endangered list. Locate an almanac that is at least ten years old, and compare the top ten endangered lists. Have the class determine through research or speculation why the list has changed.

4. One of the questions that students might ask is "What can kids do to help?" Suggestions might be:

   —Write to the legislative leaders such as area, state, and national Congressmen and Senators and ask what they are doing to help endangered species.

   —Write to the Audubon Society or another conservation group and ask what kids can do.

   —Have the class identify problems such as waterbirds getting their necks caught in the plastic that holds six-packs together. The class should generate solutions to each specific problem. In the case of the waterbirds and the six pack holder: before disposing of the holder, cut it into small pieces so the bird can't get caught in it.

   —Invite reputable members of local conservation groups to speak to the class with suggestions as to what students can do to help endangered species.

5. Since dinosaurs are such a fascinating topic to children, why not have the students investigate the various theories of their extinction, and hold a debate as to which theories seem to be most plausible.

THE FLOW TREE

INTRODUCTION

A flow tree is a delightful way to have the class remember a series of tasks or questions. It is especially helpful when the class is outdoors, and they need to focus on a series of items that need to be accomplished.

OVERVIEW

A series of cards is prepared prior to the lesson. As each item is introduced and discussed, the card for that item is added to the tree. Since the words are written on both sides of the card, the wind can turn the cards gently, and the students can still follow the line of thought. The flow tree is extremely effective indoors as well as outdoors.

    If this lesson is to be conducted outdoors, laminate the cards.

PROCEDURE

1. Identify the key points of the lesson or the order in which questions or tasks are to be accomplished.

2. Using various colors of oaktag or other heavy paper, cut out large geometric shapes. Punch a hole in the top and the bottom of the oaktag piece.

3. Write the questions, or the main points of the lesson on the varied colored pieces of paper. Make sure the questions are written on both sides of the paper.

4. Twist heavy-duty paperclips so they form an "S."

5. Create a means by which the first sign can hang. A string or wire coat hanger will work well. If outdoors, place the coat hanger in the tree before the class arrives. It looks like magic when you hang the first card on the hanger! Most kids won't see the coat hanger until the card is on it.

6. Hang each subsequent card on the previous card using the paperclips.

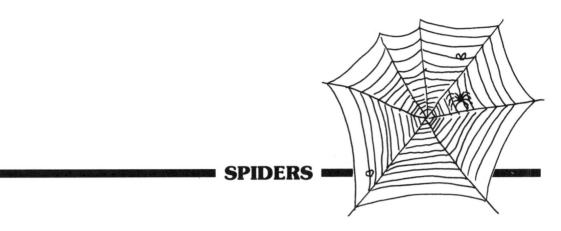

SPIDERS

INTRODUCTION

Spiders are of interest to most children, whether they claim to be frightened by them or not. The amazing arachnids are found in large numbers throughout the world. Students need to discover that spiders are helpful, fascinating, and play a very important role in controlling insect populations. Spiders play an integral part in the food web.

These activities are based in science, but they branch into problem-solving skills, critical thinking skills, math, natural history, creative writing, and art. The trick is to keep a spirit of fun alive as the students participate in the spider activities. Students coming to class wide-eyed and eager to learn is one of the best compliments that we, as teachers, can ever receive!

OVERVIEW

Several lessons are included within this unit. Students may use scientific sampling techniques to determine the number of spiders in a specified area. In another lesson, they spin giant webs and attempt to think, feel and react as spiders do. Students can attend a spider convention of their own creation, or even have a spider as a living, *temporary*, classroom attraction.

PROCEDURES

Giant Spider Web Weaving

1. Discuss with the class the ways that different spiders catch their food. Some spiders use webs, some run after their prey and catch it, some build structures to hide in and then jump out and catch their dinner, some lasso their prey, and some jump and pounce on their food. If possible, as each method is mentioned, show the class a picture or drawing of each spider and how it catches its food.

(Pictures can be found in *Ranger Rick* magazine, *National Geographic World, National Geographic*, or other nature-oriented magazines.)

2. This lesson focuses on one type of spider, the orb web weaving spider. Using an excerpt from *Charlotte's Web* discuss how an orb web weaver eats (drinks) its food.

3. Demonstrate, step by step, how the orb web weaving spider constructs a web. (Refer to the hand-out CONSTRUCT A GIANT SPIDER WEB! which you may want to pass out now.)

4. Divide the class into small groups of two or three. Take the students outdoors to a suitable, wooded area. Announce that they are about to construct their own webs. Select the boundaries within which the class will remain.

5. Remind the class that, as spiders, they want to construct their webs in a spot where there will be many insects. Later, they will need to give reasons as to why the group selected the site where their web was constructed.

6. Give each group a length of bailing twine, inexpensive rope or string and a pair of scissors. Yarn is not a good material for the web since it tends to stretch and look sloppy.

7. Students should try to construct a web that is about three meters by three meters, but the size of the finished products will probably vary greatly. You may wish to have copies of web weaving steps for some of the groups, if reinforcement is needed. (See the CONSTRUCT A GIANT SPIDER WEB sheet.)

8. Allow the students enough time to complete their webs. You should circulate among the groups providing encouragement and tips on how to proceed. Only offer help and pointers if they are requested.

9. When all webs are finished, a tour of each web is in order. As each group presents its web to the entire class, they should explain why they selected the spot that they did, how they created the web, and what they plan to catch in it. The members of the other groups evaluate the webs as they are presented. It is important to keep a sense of humor and allow the spirit of fun and pretending to prevail. Kids who aren't great web builders should still feel good about the project and enjoy the feeling of being spiders.

10. Ask the class to stay close to their webs, and look for real spiders. They'll be amazed how many they see!

11. When the lesson is completed, make sure to take down any webs that would obstruct any path or trail. If a web is out of the way, you might consider leaving it up for a while, but at some point, you should remove all webs.

12. If time allows, have the students play a game where they use their senses as real spiders do. Have one student place his/her hand on the center of one of the webs. This student is the spider waiting for its prey. The student must close his/her eyes and wait for the web to shake. Another student acts like an insect caught in the web by gently shaking one spot somewhere on the web. The "spider" has two chances to point to the exact place where the "insect" is caught in the web.

Construct A Giant Spider Web!

Spider Counting—An Estimation Experience

Taking a spider tally is a way for the class to investigate scientific sampling technique. Not only does the class learn how scientists use this method, they also discover that there really are incredible numbers of spiders in our world.

1. Take the class outdoors and have the students work in groups of two. Assign each group to one small area, approximately 5 meters by 5 meters.

2. One student acts as the spider spotter, and the other is the recorder. Their task is to tally the number of spiders they find in their area.

3. When everyone has finished counting, determine how many spiders were in the total area surveyed. Using some simple math, have the class find the average number of spiders for a 5m × 5m area.

4. Ask the class to determine the approximate number of spiders in an area that is 100m × 100m. Then 1000m × 1000m—a square kilometer.

5. Perhaps the class should also do a sampling of the number of spiders during another time of year to see if the count is different. Perhaps they should take a sampling using different terrains to discover if spiders have a preference of habitats.

Jumping Spider

The Spider Convention

The Spider Convention is exactly that…a day where all of the students pretend to be spiders attending a convention for their own kind. Students gain experience in research techniques, creative thinking, critical thinking, and problem solving skills as they prepare for the convention. The actual day of the convention is the climax of the activity. It is one of those days that students remember for many years!

1. The convention is for spiders only, so students must look like spiders in order to attend. Using spider books, encyclopedias, or observing real spiders, students create masks that make themselves look like real spiders. In Tom Walther's *A Spider Might*, there are some great spider faces that the students can use to create their masks. They also need to have the appropriate number of legs. Some might even attempt to have the appropriate body markings for their species.

2. At the convention, spider facts might be exchanged, spider books for children can be reviewed, and what's new in the spider world can be discussed.

3. Panel discussions might include topics such as "Miss Muffett, the Beginning of Bad Press" or "Strategies for Survival: Which is the Best?"

To organize these discussions, appoint four or five students to the panel, and give one of the panelists a position which he/she must defend. Make sure that the positions conflict. Appoint a moderator who will control the discussion. A plan for the discussion should be developed in advance. The plan might be similar to the following:

—Each panelist describes his/her postion for one minute.

—After each has presented his/her position, other panelists can react to what has been said by other panelists for about two minutes.

—Each panelist sums up his/her thoughts for one minute.

It is imperative that the panelists plan what points they wish to cover in advance. If everyone agrees with everyone else, or no one has any facts or creative ideas, there isn't much sense for the panel. Well-prepared members make great discussions.

4. A few weeks prior to the convention, the class creative writing assignment might be "My Scariest Close Encounter" written by each class member as if he/she were a spider. At the convention, best compositions can be read aloud to all of the assembled spiders.

5. For artistically inclined spiders, a web competition could include categories as:

most creative

most effective

most beautiful

most unusual web material

most likely to succeed

most realistic

All entries should be winners. Create new categories for each entry if necessary. Everyone should receive a ribbon or a certificate.

6. The students might create spider jokes, puns, poems, or tall tales to share at the convention.

7. If you are planning snacks, have the class decide on what spider-like foods should be prepared. Do raisins look somewhat like dead flies? What else could be consumed? Grasshopper shaped cookies, perhaps. Whatever the beverage, straws are a must!

Possibilities for convention activities are unlimited! Let your imagination run wild. Involve the class with most of the planning. Get your administrators, librarians, art teachers, home economics teachers, and parents into the act.

8. The day after the convention, as the children are evaluating the event, try to discuss why a real spider convention would not take place. It's probable the students will have learned enough about spiders to know that they would devour one another.

Spider Visits the Classroom

You may wish to keep a spider in the room as a living display. If you choose to do so, please remember that you must show respect for your spider as well as all living things. Once you have finished your study, the spider should be returned to the place where it was found. It is also important that the class treat their spider with respect.

1. When you find a spider that you think will make a suitable guest for your classroom, identify it to make sure that it is not one of the two poisonous spiders found in North America. There are hundreds of spiders; only two are considered poisonous.

> —*The black widow* is a shiny black spider, with a red hourglass on its underside.

> —*The brown recluse* is a brown spider with a violin-shaped marking on its abdomen. Both are relatively rare, but please use caution when selecting your classroom guest.

A note of caution: Check to see if any student has an allergy to spiders or spider bites.

2. If your spider is an orb web weaver, you can place it on a rock that is in the center of a large tub of water. Make sure that a portion of the rock is above the water line. Place two or three long, thin poles or sticks so they touch the rock and extend straight up into the air. The spider will use the sticks to anchor its web, and the class will have the chance to watch their guest in action! If your classroom doesn't have lots of flying things that spiders like to eat, you may have to catch some and throw them into the web to provide food for your guest.

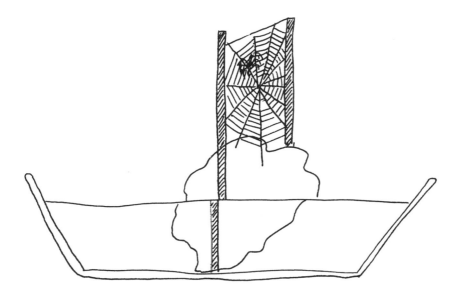

3. In case your spider is not an orb web weaver, you can prepare a terrarium for it. Cover the top with fine mesh screening, not glass. Make sure there is a supply of fresh water, (a bottle cap full, changed daily, is plenty) a few plants, some rocks and pebbles, and a few insects for food.

4. When the study is done, return the spider to the outdoors where it can live happily ever after, as long as you return it when the weather isn't freezing!

RESOURCES, BOOKS ABOUT SPIDERS

Brinckloe, Julie. *The Spider Web*. Garden City: Doubleday & Company, Inc., 1974.

> In this wordless book, students can see, step by step, how a spider goes about spinning an orb web.

Graham, Margaret Bloy. *Be Nice to Spiders*. New York: Harper & Row, 1967.

> This gentle story points out the beneficial habits of spiders.

Levi, Herbert W., Levi, Lorna L., and Zim, Herbert S. *A Guide to Spiders and Their Kin*. New York: Golden Press, 1968.

> This is an inexpensive guide to identifying spiders with information about each type of spider. It is easy for students to use, with colorful, accurate illustrations.

McNulty, Faith. *The Lady and the Spider*. New York: Harper & Row, 1987.

> A garden spider's daily life is highlighted in this delicately illustrated book. The actions and reactions of spiders are realistically portrayed.

Ross, Tony. *I'm Coming to Get You!* New York: Greenwillow Books, 1984.

> This book is not specifically about spiders—it deals with facing unrealistic fears. This might be useful with students who have a hard time overcoming a fear of spiders.

Walther, Tom. *A Spider Might*. San Francisco/New York: Sierra Club Books/Charles Scribner's Sons, 1978.

> This well-written, fact-filled book is a great resource if you are going to do the Spider Convention activity. It has accurate information, pictures of spider faces, drawings of spiders, silhouettes indicating their real sizes, and an annotated bibliography.

White, E.B. *Charlotte's Web*. New York: Harper & Row, 1952.

> Although the story is fictional, the description of how Charlotte (the spider) eats is a good one.

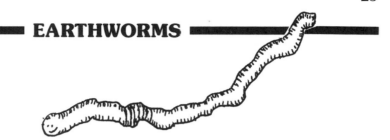

EARTHWORMS

INTRODUCTION

The earthworm is a delightful classroom animal that is easily cared for. Prior to this classroom study, most children have not closely observed earthworms in the wild or in captivity. Students are fascinated when they have the opportunity to study the harmless earthworms in the classroom. At first a few students may react with the traditional "YUCK," but by the end of the study, the class will appreciate the deeds of such valuable friends of the earth.

OVERVIEW

Students study the earthworm by carefully noting its behavior. Students observe the earthworms, and create an earthworm home. The class discovers how earthworms help to make the soil richer as they discover more about their eating habits. They design "race tracks" for the earthworms—which in reality is a study of earthworm locomotion, as well as earthworms' reaction to light. Students set up their own experiments to determine some aspect of earthworm behavior.

PROCEDURES

The Great Earthworm Hunt

1. Prior to beginning the earthworm study, ask the class to make a drawing of what they think an earthworm looks like. Next, ask each student to write a short paragraph about earthworms. The paragraph should describe an earthworm's physical characteristics, what earthworms eat, how they move around, where they live, and any other thoughts that might be appropriate.

2. On the day the study is to begin, bring a shovel and a bucket to class and announce that the "Great Earthworm Hunt" is about to take place. Before leaving the classroom, ask the students:

   —where earthworms might be found

   —whether or not earthworms show any evidence of themselves above ground

   —which areas near the school might be the most productive places to dig

3. Using the students' replies, proceed to the areas that the class has suggested. If they know about earthworms, those places will be areas where there is vegetation, trees, and loose soil. Earthworms eat the leaf litter and make the soil rich through this process, so you'll find them where their food supply is!

   Look for earthworm castings as evidence that the worms are below. Earthworm castings look like squiggly piles of dirt somewhat like small anthills. The castings are deposits left by the worms when they come to the surface at night.

   NOTE: If you can't find earthworms no matter how hard you try, even if you are looking in the right type of area, you can order earthworms from garden supply shops. You can also ask the students to bring some in from home. Kids usually know where to find earthworms!

4. When you find earthworms, place them gently in a clean bucket or large, clean, gallon size plastic container. Make sure to get lots of soil with the worms so they have a place to hide, live, and eat while they are in your care.

5. Once you return to the room with the earthworms, or the next time you have science class, have the class study the worms carefully. Place the worms on a clean surface and ask the class to *really* look at them.

   Depending on the individuals in the class, you can either have the class divide into small study groups, or allow each student to study his/her own worm.

6. Once again review the questions that you asked of the class before you set out on the "Great Earthworm Hunt." Discuss the student's discoveries about earthworms.

   Where are earthworms found?

   Do earthworms show any evidence of themselves above ground?

   Where nearby might earthworms be found?

7. The next time the class has a chance to study the worms, ask the class to draw the worms as they observe them. When the sketches are complete, ask the students to write a paragraph describing the physical characteristics of earthworms. Add some new questions for the class to answer:

   How are worms able to move around?

   Do worms have eyes?

   Are all the worm's segments the same?

8. As the class finds the answers to the questions through direct observation, add more questions that are a bit more thought-provoking, such as:

   What do they eat?

   Why do they always seem to come to the surface after a rainstorm?

   Do they prefer to be in the dark or the light?

(See EARTHWORMS: AN INVESTIGATION worksheet.)

EARTHWORM
AN INVESTIGATION...

1. Where are earthworms found?

2. Do earthworms show any evidence of themselves above ground?

3. Where can we find earthworms nearby?

4. How are earthworms able to move around?

5. Do worms have eyes?

6. Are all the worm's segments the same?

7. What do they eat?

8. Why do they come to the surface after a rainstorm?

9. Do they prefer to be in the dark or the light?

9. Discuss other questions and answers as they arise from the observations. You might want to graphically demonstrate how the earthworms move soil by creating an earthworm home.
(See BUILDING AN EARTHWORM HOME)

10. As soon as the earthworm home has been completed, ask the class to make predictions about what will happen when the "Earthworm Home" is checked in a week.

Building an Earthworm Home

1. Thoroughly clean a gallon-sized glass jar or a terrarium.

2. Spread a layer of clean gravel on the bottom.

3. Alternate layers of light colored sand, rich moist soil, and leaf litter in the terrarium or glass jar so that each layer is about ½-inch thick. Make sure that the layers are distinct.

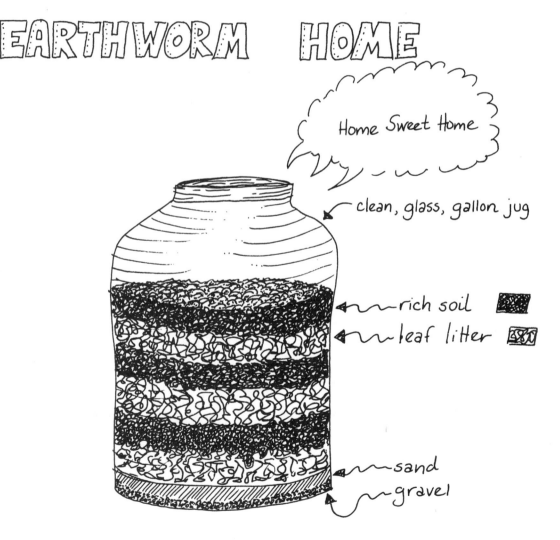

4. Put some lettuce, a small piece of tomato and other foods on top of the soil to see if the earthworms will eat any of it.

5. Add a few earthworms and cover the glass part of the jar/terrarium with black paper. (If you forget to do this, they won't come close to the edges; they like the dark!)

6. Tightly stretch cheesecloth across the top and secure it.

7. After a week or so, remove the black paper and notice how the worms have mixed the soil. Notice the lettuce, tomato and other foods that were left on top of the soil.

8. After another week, check the "Earthworm Home."

> Notice which food was left on top of the soil.
>
> Discuss how the worms have moved the layers.
>
> Look to see if the earthworms have left castings on the top soil layers.
>
> Ask the class whether or not the "Earthworm Home" reflects what probably happens in real life.

If for some reason not much has changed, cover the whole thing again and wait for two weeks, then check the home again.

Which Surfaces Do Earthworms Prefer?

1. The students will probably have noticed many of the earthworms' characteristics by now. Have the class determine which surfaces the worms seem to prefer. Ask the class how an experiment can be set up which determines the surface of preference. The class should suggest surfaces which are smooth, soft, bumpy, scratchy, rough, hard, etc., for testing.

2. Remind the class that it is important to act as scientists in this experiment. The only factor which is variable should be the surface. All other factors should remain the same.

3. Ask the class whether to use the same worm over and over, or should many worms be used? Why?

4. What will determine whether or not the earthworms "like" a surface or not?

> Speed of crawling?
>
> Whether the worm stays on the surface for any length of time?
>
> How quickly the worm leaves the surface?

5. What should each surface tested be placed on?

> A table with dirt all around the testing surface?
>
> A table with nothing but the table top around the surface?
>
> Outdoors on the ground, with the prospect of freedom as the incentive?
>
> Outdoors with the different surfaces lined up one next to another?

6. Will the results be different if the experiment is conducted on different days? What other factors must be considered?

7. Have the class develop the best experiment to discover which surface earthworms prefer. Once they have the information as to surface preference, they can use that information for the next experiment.

Earthworm Races

1. What designs will be most effective to race earthworms? Ask the students to create designs for earthworm racetracks. Once the designs have been completed, students share their individual creations. The class should evaluate each track as to its practical implementation, safety for the earthworms, good design, and any other factors. Select one or two designs that the class feels will best meet the needs for the experiment.

2. The class also needs to determine what will motivate an earthworm to move along the racetrack.

   • One factor can be the surface of the track.
   • Another factor can be the earthworm's preference of light or dark. Will the earthworms move more rapidly if a bright light is shining on one section of the track, and a dark space is opposite the light?
   • Will the earthworm be able to find a dark space that is not exactly opposite the light, but to one side?
   • If the amount of light is increased, will the worms crawl faster to the dark?

3. After the class has determined the best way to set up the experiments, allow them to conduct them.

   NOTE: It is very important that the class always remember to treat the earthworms with respect and never cause them to be harmed in anyway. A reverence for all living things must be a part of the handling of classroom animals.

4. Ask the class if they can think of any other experiments that can safely be conducted with the earthworms. Examples might include:

   • Earthworm food preference.
   • Do earthworms prefer one type of soil? (sandy, clay, humus, rocky, dry, damp)
   • Will an earthworm avoid types of soil if afforded the opportunity?

   Have the class set up the suggested experiments, always making sure that the experiments are conducted as a scientist would.

   When you have completed your study make sure that all of the earthworms are returned to the place where they were captured. It is important to show respect for all living things, worms included!

   Once again, ask the class to draw a picture of an earthworm, as you did at the onset of this activity. Have the students compare their first drawings with the final drawings.

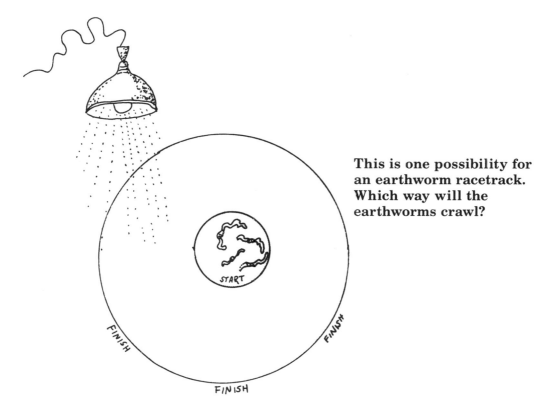

This is one possibility for an earthworm racetrack. Which way will the earthworms crawl?

■■■ BIRDS AND BIRD FEEDERS OF ALL SORTS ■■■

INTRODUCTION

Turn a craft project, like making bird feeders from recycled milk cartons, into a science lesson that lasts throughout the school year!

OVERVIEW

Students focus on the special adaptations of birds' beaks and feet as they study the way in which birds obtain their food. Students design and create bird feeders appropriate for the feeding habits of specific birds.

This is a great fall activity, since the class can reap the rewards of attracting birds to the feeders throughout the year. Please make sure that once the birds are used to the feeder that it is maintained throughout the year. In places with cold winters when little food is available, birds become dependent on the feeder. When spring rolls around, and food is plentiful again, the feeder can be set aside, but not before. Feeders require a commitment for the entire winter, even through winter vacations.

PROCEDURE

How Birds Obtain Their Food

1. Discuss the types of foods that different birds eat. (seeds, worms, nectar, acorns, beetles, grubs, ants, caterpillars, berries, fish, mice, etc.)
2. Prior to this lesson, collect several photographs and drawings of birds that are found locally. The pictures and drawings should include varied kinds of birds, including songbirds, waterbirds, marsh and shorebirds, upland gamebirds, and birds of prey.

Need Help?—Audubon Society to the Rescue!

If you feel that you don't know much about your bird population, a good place to inquire is the local chapter of the Audubon Society. They are always happy to help provide information to teachers. Often they will conduct educational programs for schools, provide free literature for classroom use, sponsor educational workshops for teachers or even provide scholarships to send teachers to attend Audubon Camp.

Other places to inquire might include:

Nearby environmental education centers

Raptor rehabilitation facilities

The science department of nearby high schools, colleges, or universities

Camps

Fellow teachers—you never know who might be an avid bird watcher!

A great book that will provide information on the diets of various birds is *American Wildlife and Plants—A Guide to Wildlife Food Habits*, written by Alexander C. Martin, Herbert S. Zim, and Arnold L. Nelson. This paperback should be in every school library.

3. Ask the class what special adaptations birds have for getting their food. Try to have the different types of local birds in the picture display. Have the class focus on the variety of ways that different species use their feet and beaks.
4. Create a list of things that each bird eats and how that bird accomplishes eating it. For example, the red-tailed hawk eats mice by swooping down on the mouse and grabbing it in its talons. The blue jay eats acorns by piercing the nut with its sharp bill. The yellow-shafted flicker eats ants by digging in the ground with its pointed bill and pulls ants up using its raspy tongue. The evening grossbeak cracks seed shells with its strong short beak.
5. Ask the class to divide into small groups with two or three students per group. Provide an assortment of recycled materials such as empty milk cartons, juice containers, paper towel rolls, scrap paper, scraps of fabric, string, ribbon and any other recycled materials. You also should provide glue, scissors, tape, staplers, and paper clips. Ask each group to turn one of its members into a bird. The students should decide what food their bird eats and then they must create feet, wings and a beak for their bird.

Name _____ Date _____

BIRD ADAPTATIONS

Name of Bird	Food	Beak	Feet	Other

As always, circulate as the groups are creating. Provide encouragement and keep them on task! Provide no answers, but ask questions that will allow the students to solve their own problems.

6. As each group presents its "bird," make sure that its beak, feet wings, and other features are explained. You might wish to award each group with a special ribbon. Winners might be categorized such as "Best Bird," "Most Efficient Beak," "Feet That Are Most Appropriate," "Most Creative Explanation," or similar categories. Try to have a ribbon for each group so that everyone feels successful.

7. As a review, discuss the types of adaptations that the different birds demonstrated. A chart modeled on the BIRD ADAPTATIONS worksheet might be created on the board to enhance the discussion. Students can use the chart to take notes.

BIRD ADAPTATIONS

PROCEDURE

A Duck Feeder?

1. Now that the class is focused on the adaptations needed for birds to obtain food, have the class decide on five or six local birds that are very different from each other. Possibilities might include hummingbird, robin, chickadee, mallard, nuthatch, turkey vulture, osprey, red-tailed hawk, wild turkey, canada goose, yellow-shafted flicker, or snowy owl.

2. After the class has selected five or six local birds, have each student secretly select one of the local birds. As an independent assignment, each student designs a feeder that will work for the bird that they have selected. As a part of the assignment, each student must determine the foods that will be placed in the feeder. With some birds, the feeder might not have to be maintained all winter, as that species migrates elsewhere for the cold season.

3. When each student has completed his/her assignment, each design should be shared with the group. The design should be simple enough that it can be constructed by the student from recycled materials, easy to re-stock, and appropriate for the bird.

4. Once again, have the class create small working groups. The basis for each group should be a desire to create a feeder for one type of bird. Allow each group to create one or more feeders for the selected bird.

5. Each group must also create a proposal for their feeder which includes all information requested on THE PROPOSED BIRD FEEDER worksheet. As the groups work on their proposals, make sure that you circulate to each group. Watch for proposals that don't reflect real possibilities. Each must be workable as well as practical. If parts of a proposal are not practical, quietly point out the reasons why those areas need to be rewritten.

THE
PROPOSED BIRD FEEDER
OF:

NAME _____   NAME _____

NAME _____   NAME _____

..... Please submit a sketch of the feeder, and a list of ..... materials needed to construct it with this proposal.

★ Which birds will be attracted to your planned feeder?

_____

★★ What food will be placed in the feeder?

★ Where will the feeder be placed? How will it be secured?

_____

★★ Where will the food come from?

_____

★ Will it be necessary to maintain the feeder throughout the winter? If so, who will be responsible for maintaining the feeder over winter vacations?

_____

★★ Who will keep records on which animals are attracted to the feeder, the amount of food consumed, and other details?

_____

★ Who will make any necessary repairs or modifications on the feeder?

_____

☐ other information: _____

☐ _____

6. Allow each group to present the completed feeder and its proposal to the assembled class. Ask the audience to help evaluate each feeder and the accompanying proposal in terms of practicality, efficiency, and dependability.

Categories for feeders should be explained to the class prior to the presentations.

> ***Working Model***—All feeders that qualify as working models should be placed in service.

> ***Display Model***—Feeders that are based on a good idea and/or a creative concept but are impractical to put into service can be categorized as a "display model."

Feeders that do not meet the standards for either category should be reworked until they qualify for the "display model" category or the "working model" category. Make sure that concrete suggestions are offered to those groups so that they can quickly succeed in their efforts.

7. When evaluating the project, make sure that the class develops a means of monitoring each feeder which is placed in use to determine its effectiveness. Criteria might include:

> —The number of birds actually observed using the feeder, as well as other animals that use the feeder. (Squirrels need to eat too!)

> —How easily the feeder is restocked.

> —How well the feeder holds up throughout the season.

> —Modifications that would make the feeder more effective.

8. At the end of the school year, or when the feeders are no longer in use, discuss the project and its effectiveness to determine a better way to approach the project. Students may offer incredible insights to make the whole project more effective. When they know that their opinion counts, they truly offer good ideas.

EXTENSIONS

A group of students once met all the criteria with a turkey vulture feeder. The feeder consisted of a wooden platform in a tree, about 10 feet off the ground. The food supply was provided by various road kills. Since turkey vultures migrate to lower latitudes for the winter, winter feeding was unnecessary. A project that is as creative as this one requires special safety and legal considerations before it is approved as a "Working Model" feeder.

> —Make sure that it is legal to remove road kills without a permit in your state. In my state, it is necessary to have a permit to do so. It is not difficult to obtain the permit when the purposes for removal are educational.

> —Notify building administrators as to the nature of the feeder just in case a parent has a question or two.

> —Students who collect road kills need to use plastic gloves when

handling road kills. It is also a good idea to place the road kill in a double plastic bag that can be sealed tightly.

—Pedestrian safety must come first. Students may not take any risks when obtaining the road kill. We don't want to add them to the feeder!

—When restocking the feeder, the tree climber must use caution as he/she climbs the tree.

FOOD WEBS

INTRODUCTION

We are all a part of the food web. John Muir wrote, "Everything is hitched to everything else." The following activities encourage children of all ages to experience the food chain for themselves.

FOOD WEB STAMP COLLECTING

OVERVIEW

Students begin this activity by researching common animals in an uncommon way. Each student is assigned an animal that can be found within the local ecosystem. The researcher determines what foods his/her animal eats and what, if anything, eats the animal. The animal's lifestyle must also be investigated. After the mini reports have been completed, the collecting game begins! Each student needs to complete a food web using stamps created by other students. Adding a time limit forces students to work quickly, yet everyone is able to succeed!

PROCEDURE

1. This lesson begins with a lottery. Students select one piece of paper from a hat, box, or some other container. Each piece of paper has the name of an animal found within the local ecosystem.

2. After everyone has an animal, announce that each student needs to find out what the animal eats, what eats it, and how that animal's lifestyle determines what the animal eats. For example, frogs live near ponds, so they tend to eat pond-dwelling insects, and owls hunt at night, so they eat nocturnal rodents. Some caterpillars are paralyzed by wasps, which then lay eggs on the caterpillar, which eventually serves as food for the newly-emerged wasps.

3. After two or three class periods of research, students should be ready to present their findings. Have them report orally to their class. The class should take short

Name_____   Date_____

NOTES ON MINI REPORTS:

ANIMAL	WHAT IT EATS	WHAT EATS IT	OTHER FACTS	FOOD WEB PLACE

notes or fill in the NOTES ON MINI REPORTS worksheet. This prepares students for the next phase of the project.

4. Students need to categorize each animal as a **primary consumer, secondary consumer, third order consumer**, or scavenger. This can be accomplished as a class discussion project, an individual homework assignment, or a combination of both. Before proceeding, though, make sure that all students have the correct information.

5. Distribute the FOOD WEB STAMPS sheet that has the nine blank squares. Ask the students to draw a picture of their animal in each square. (If they are worried about their art work, let them label the animal.)

6. Distribute the FOOD WEB game sheet. Announce that the students have a set amount of time to trade with one another for the squares to complete one food web on their sheets. The food web sheet must be accurate. One full school day is usually enough for the students to complete the sheets. Trading can take place in the halls, during lunch, or any free time. However, students may *not* trade during other classes or interrupt learning in any way.

7. When the students have found animals for their sheets, they are given two blank squares to correctly draw a producer and a decomposer to complete the sheet. But students need to use caution before they can draw a producer. They need to know which plants their primary consumer eats. They can't have rabbits trying to eat duckweed!

8. When all webs have been completed, and handed in, discuss each completed food web with the class.

If you live in the Deciduous Forest biome, the animals that might be used for the food web are:

meadow mouse	red-tailed hawk	dragonfly
chipmunk	black bear	gnat
mole	great horned owl	bass
earthworm	grey wolf	shad
spider	raccoon	pickerel
housefly	turkey	caddisfly
white-tailed deer	turkey vulture	leech
cottontail rabbit	crow	mountain lion
skunk	red squirrel	black fly
leopard frog	grasshopper	bald eagle

Name_____ Date_____

FOOD WEB STAMPS

Please draw your animal accurately in each one of these squares. If you are worried that people won't know what your drawing is, please label it! When you have finished, cut the squares apart. If someone needs one of your squares to complete his/her food web, please give one to him/her. Make sure you discuss what your animal needs to survive, so the web is accurate.

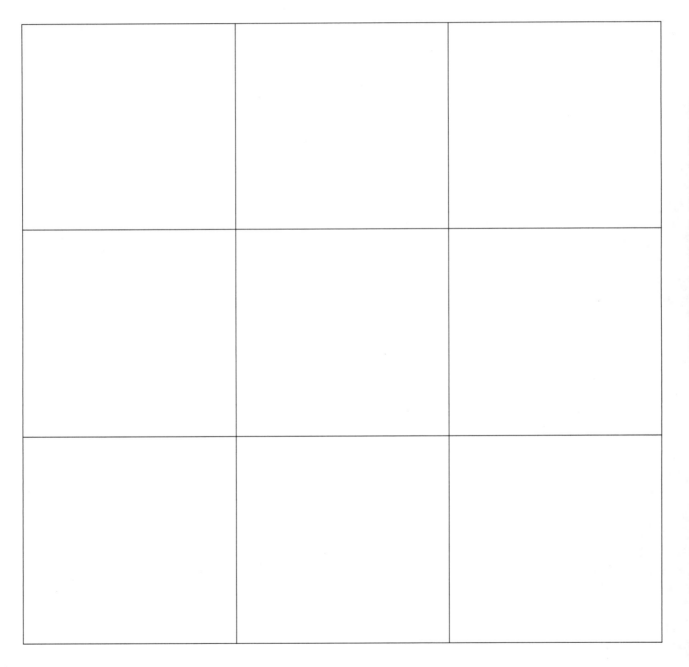

Name_____ Date_____

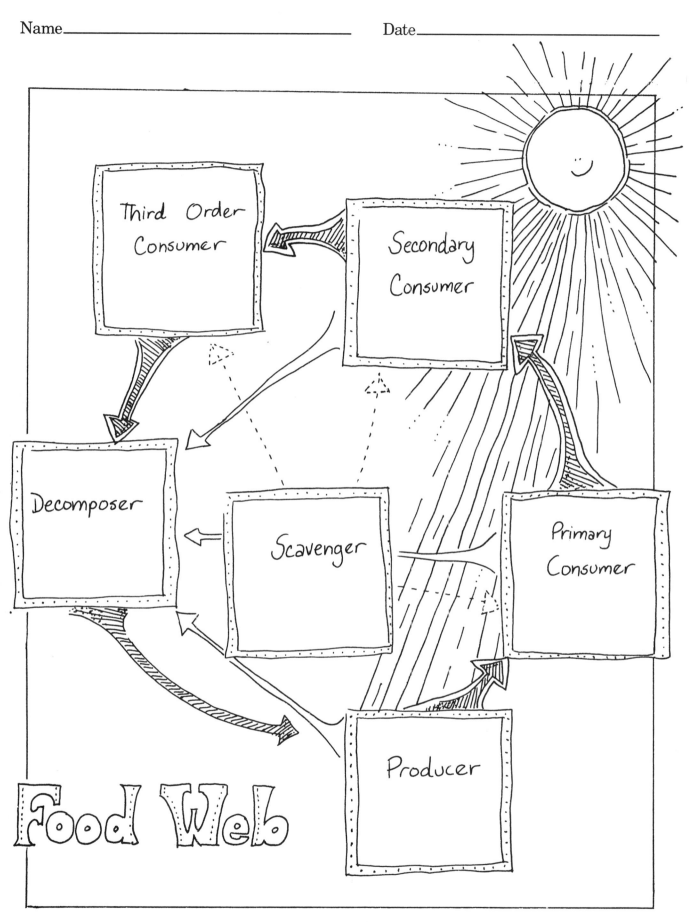

Third Order Consumer

Secondary Consumer

Decomposer

Scavenger

Primary Consumer

Producer

Food Web

mosquito	monarch butterfly	red fox
carpenter ant	bat	flying squirrel
beaver	blue jay	osprey

Some animals require specific plants in order to survive. For example, the monarch butterfly caterpillar must eat milkweed in order to survive. Make sure that the students have the right plants in their web so that their animal is able to survive.

CARTOON FOOD CHAINS

INTRODUCTION

A great book about food chains that you might want to share with the students is *Cricket in the Grass* by Philip Van Soelen (Sierra Club Books/Charles Scribner's Sons, San Francisco/New York, 1979.) *Cricket in the Grass* is a series of pen and ink illustrations of food webs. The only words are found in the back of the book, for explanation if needed. The drawings accurately detail several food webs, beginning with, what else?—a cricket in the grass that is eaten by a toad. The toad is then eaten by a snake, the snake is captured by a red-tailed hawk, who loses a feather which floats to earth and lands near an oak log which is decomposing with help from fungus, bark beetles, and so on. The cycle continues, involving all sorts of habitats. The book ends, appropriately, with man.

In case you can't locate a copy of the book, a great way to find a copy is to use your public library's inter-library loan service. Most libraries offer this service for any book found in the volumes of *Books in Print*.

OVERVIEW

Even if you do not have the chance to use *Cricket in the Grass* a great activity is to have the students create their own drawings of food chains.

PROCEDURE

1. Place the students in groups of three or four, and ask them to design a sequence for one food web. For example: a mouse eats a wild strawberry, a snake eats the mouse, the snake is eaten by an owl. You might have the students give the drawings a sense of mystery and escape by having one animal fail to catch its prey, only to have the prey eaten by a different animal.

2. Each student then draws one or two of the pictures for the series. Students should try to draw the background objects so that they look similar. It is also a good idea for all the students in one group to use the same medium. It does help to give each series a sharp, well-thought-out look.

3. When all of the students have finished, have the students share the series of drawings with the class, explaining what eats what in their food chain.

4. The food chains should be displayed so that students can look closely at the completed chains. In many of them, students have taken great pains to incorporate small details which otherwise might be overlooked.

Helpful Hints

Should you run into students who are squeamish and upset at the prospect of animals eating other animals, one of the very best explanations that can be used is, "He's not mean, he's just hungry." A class discussion should help the students to come to a better understanding of the realities of the world in which we all live.

Some children might want to draw a great deal of blood and gore with their pictures. You might remind them that animals must be very careful when capturing prey so they don't expend too much energy. Animals usually kill their prey with minimal bloodshed. Ask any student who has drawn a picture that you feel is too gory to do it over again without the blood.

There are a great number of activities which simulate food webs and how animals survive. Some additional games that can be utilized are "Quick Frozen Critters" and "How Many Bears." Both of these activities may be found in the *Project Wild* Elementary edition. *Project Wild* is a joint project of the Western Association of Fish and Wildlife Agencies and the Western Regional Environmental Education Council, copyrighted in 1983.

PESTICIDE DEBATE

INTRODUCTION

One way to generate interest in the issues of pesticides is a great activity in which the students take part in a debate. The students develop skills that they will need as adults. They are actively involved in researching a topic and then processing that which they have researched into a logical, factual argument.

OVERVIEW

Students take part in an active debate in which they must defend their views.

PROCEDURE

1. The parts in this debate are as follows:

the pesticide user, Farmer Smith

the animals affected by the pesticide

the pesticide manufacturer

the people opposed to pesticides

a moderator

a judge, who will make a decision based on the arguments of the groups

2. Tell the class that they will participate in a simulation of a real problem. Farmer Smith has decided to use more pesticides on his corn crop because his corn this year had more insect damage than ever. The animals of the local food web are outraged. They have brought the farmer to court to ask that he be prevented from adding more pesticide to the farm.

3. Divide the class into the various groups.

4. Allow the groups to have two or three days to prepare their arguments, research facts, and create charts, graphs, and other visual aids.

5. On the day of the presentation:

Allow each group to make a brief two minute statement.

After all of the statements have been completed, a group may respond to any of the statements in the opening.

Discussion should be limited to factual information, and emotional responses should be limited by the moderator.

Each group should have the opportunity to defend its position if another group specifically addresses one of its arguments.

At the end of the 20 minute discussion time, each group has two minutes to sum up its position and refute things the other groups have declared.

6. The judge weighs all of the arguments, and makes judgment as to whether or not Farmer Smith may put more pesticides on his corn.

7. With this activity, remind students that in real cases involving such an issue, emotional arguments will not make any difference in a judge's ruling. The only thing that counts are the facts. Graphs, charts, research and hard facts are the deciding factors. They need to prove their case with concrete realities.

8. Compromise is also one of the realities of such an issue. After the judge has made a ruling, the class may wish to discuss methods by which a compromise can be reached.

Currently there is much attention focused on farming with fewer chemicals, which can save farmers a great deal of money and reduce environmental damage. Methods by which they use fewer or no chemicals are called by several names, including regenerative farming, sustainable farming, low-input farming, integrated pest management, or organic farming. These terms may be helpful to the students in their research.

The Rodale Press (33 East Minor St., Emmaus, PA 18049) is actively involved with the concept of "Regenerative Farming." You might want to contact them and request information. The United States Department of Agriculture has recently changed their position on the same issue. You might wish to send a letter to them asking where they stand now.

State and county extension services that are usually connected with state universities also have information on the latest techniques in farming and are always very helpful in answering questions on current trends.

The *New York Times* of Sunday August 23, 1987 had an informative article, "Farming Without Chemicals: Age-Old Technologies Becoming State of Art." It clearly describes new farming trends. It might be worth the effort to go to the library and look up the article on microfiche.

FOOD WEB MOBILE

INTRODUCTION

Yet another way to have students see the realities of the food web is to construct a class food web pyramid. This activity visually demonstrates the reasons for the numbers of animals and plants in the real food webs of the world.

OVERVIEW

Students create mobiles of the food web pyramid.

PROCEDURE

1. Begin with a class discussion that focuses on whether there is a difference in the numbers of things in each category of the food web. Are there more primary consumers than secondary consumers? Are there more secondary consumers than third order consumers?

2. Have the class brainstorm the typical animals found where they live. On the board, begin a pyramid diagram of the local food web beginning with two or three of the third order consumers. Next add to the diagram, five or six of the second order consumers upon which the listed third order consumers would eat. Determine what the second order consumers would eat, and add those first order consumers to the diagram. Finally, have the students list the plants that are eaten by the listed primary consumers.

3. Ask each student to select one of the animals/plants listed on the board. Have them draw and cut out their animal or plant. Drawings should be on both sides, since this is a mobile! All animals and plants should have one hole punched at the top of it and one at the bottom. (To reinforce the holes, put a strip of tape on each side of the animal/plant BEFORE punching the hole.)

4. Hang one strip from the ceiling for each third order consumer. Attach each to the string, and add a piece of string to the bottom of each third order consumer.

FOOD WEB MOBILES

▭ producer
○ primary consumer
◇ secondary consumer
△ third order consumer
∪ scavenger
∞ decomposer

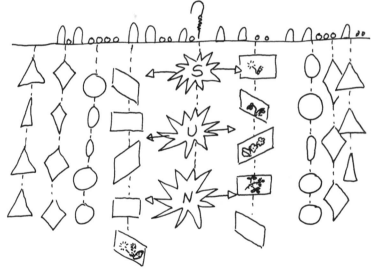

Attach a piece of coat hanger, a ruler or some other rigid, light weight strip to each string.

5. Attach the second order consumers to the pieces of coat hanger. Continue to add pieces of coat hangers and attach the primary consumers and once again, add strings and pieces of coat hangers completing the mobile with the primary consumers.

6. Have the class determine where the sun, the scavengers, and the decomposers fit into their food web mobile.

FOOD WEB GAME

INTRODUCTION

The Food Web Game is a game that introduces the students to the basic concept of energy flow and the interdependence of animals in an ecosystem. Learners are actively involved in collecting all the necessary components of a food web. Later they create their own detailed food web to play a harder version of this game.

OVERVIEW

Students are divided into groups and each group receives a "hand" of food web cards. The object is for the group to trade cards with other groups until they have a complete food web. Students must know what components make up the food web in order to be successful!

PROCEDURE

1. Make 48 cards using the following information:

    Total Deck: 48 5" × 7" file cards

    6 cards labeled "sun"

    10 cards labeled "producer"

    6 cards labeled "primary consumer"

    6 cards labeled "secondary consumer"

    6 cards labeled "third order consumer"

    6 cards labeled "scavenger"

    6 cards labeled "decomposer"

    1 card labeled "people"

    1 card labeled "pollution"

Depending on how creative or artistic you want to be, you may:

    just write the words *on one side* of a 5" × 7" card.

    you can embellish the 5" × 7" cards by writing each word and cutting out appropriate pictures from magazines.

    draw pictures of your own design on each card.

    duplicate the pages at the end of this chapter, and mount them on cards.

However you decide to proceed, make sure that the cards are thick enough so that the words written on one side can't be seen on the other side. After the cards are completed, laminate them. If your school doesn't have a laminating machine, use clear shelf paper.

2. You should create cards so that they all represent one biome. The suggestions

that follow are all found in the deciduous forest biome. If you live in a desert, why not create a desert version? This introduction to the food web should include plants and animals that are familiar to your students—so adapt the lists to fit YOUR habitat!

Deciduous Forest Food Web Cards

Sun (6 cards)

Producer (10 cards)
  black raspberry plant
  strawberry plant
  red sweet clover
  oak tree
  grape vine
  ox eye daisy
  milkweed
  Queen Anne's lace
  elderberry bush
  poison ivy

Primary Consumer (6 cards)
  chipmunk
  chickadee
  grasshopper
  cricket
  field mouse
  caterpillar

Secondary Consumer (6 cards)
  praying mantis
  woodpecker
  leopard frog
  garter snake
  Baltimore oriole
  jumping spider

Third Order Consumer (6 cards)
  raccoon
  red shouldered hawk
  hog nosed snake
  red fox
  barn owl
  American kestrel

Scavenger (6 cards)
  crow
  black carrion beetle
  turkey vulture
  house fly
  sexton beetle
  coyote

Decomposer (6 cards)
  slime mold
  mushroom
  bacteria
  turkey tail fungus
  artist conch
  puff ball

People (1 card)
  A picture of a person (Looking mysterious, as if he/she has a secret.)

Pollution (1 card)
  A picture of a factory spewing out smoke, or a dump, or a garbage-filled lake.

3. When you are ready to play, divide the class into six groups. Explain that the object of the game is to create a food web. A complete food web consists of:

> sun
> producer
> primary consumer
> secondary consumer
> third order consumer
> scavenger
> decomposer

4. At the onset of the game, each group receives one pile of cards. Since most piles of cards won't have a winning hand, the students need to exchange cards with other groups. They do this by sending one representative to the center of the room (groups are all around the sides of the room) and trading their unwanted cards with another group.

5. Each group can only trade with a group that wants to trade the same number of cards. As the swaps take place, neither group knows what they are getting until the trader returns to the group and the group looks at new cards together.

6. When a group has a complete food web, they shout "FOOD WEB!" and all trading stops, as this group proves to the other groups that they indeed do have a complete food web. If they don't, trading continues until one group is successful.

7. The winning group gets 100 points. The class will want to play several rounds. You may wish to keep score on a blackboard or on a large piece of paper so everyone can see how everyone else is doing.

8. Point out that when each group receives their cards, they should notice that they have eight cards, yet only seven cards are needed to win. The reason that they have extra cards is that there are two special cards in the deck: people and pollution.

   The people card is sometimes helpful to the food web, so if a group has the people card, they can use it as a "wild card" to replace any card that they are missing. BUT, if a group has the people card, and another group completes their food web first, 50 points will be deducted from their score. Should the group with the people card complete the whole food web, not using the people card as a wild card, they receive 200 points for winning!

   The pollution card is always bad, and whichever group has the card when the game is done, loses 50 points.

   The people card and the pollution card may be traded just as the other cards are traded.

9. When everyone understands the rules, shuffle the cards and deal out six piles of cards on a table. After all the piles are complete, invite one representative from each group to come and select one pile of cards.

10. The groups work quickly and quietly to determine which cards they want to

trade. When they are ready to trade, one representative holds the cards to his/her chest and walks to the center of the room.

11. When in the center, he/she announces the number of cards that the group is trading. "TWO...TWO...TWO" or "THREE...THREE...THREE," until a trading partner is found. No group should be forced to trade with any other group. (If one group knows that they just traded the pollution card to another group, they don't want to be forced into a trade where they get it back right away!)

12. After each game is completed, tally the scores, and discuss game playing strategies that the different groups use. For example: Groups that show no emotion upon discovering that they have just received the pollution card, have a better chance of trading it to another group than those groups that moan and screech when they see the card.

EXTENSIONS

A Harder Version of the Food Web Game

1. After the class has an understanding of the food web, select one biome and ask each group to create a set of eight cards that indicates *a real food web* in that biome.

2. Each group will need to do some real research to determine which things depend on which in a real food web.

3. When all of the cards are completed, each group presents their cards to the other groups.

4. Play the Food Web Game once again, using the same rules, EXCEPT the food web that is completed must be a real one. That doesn't mean that there can't be pieces of one group's web and another's mixed together, as long as the group can prove that their web is accurate.

5. Students may challenge the accuracy of a team's food web. It is up to both teams to undertake the research to prove the web either accurate or inaccurate using a *printed reference*. (I KNOW that a frog doesn't eat crickets is not an acceptable challenge.) Due to the challenge process, it is imperative that resources are available in the classroom. A time limit for each challenge is a good idea. Give a group 3 or 4 minutes to either prove or disprove a contested web.

6. If the class really gets into the game, have the groups make up food webs from other biomes.

Name That Biome

Create a food web from a specific biome, post it on the bulletin board and have the class deduce which biome that food web represents.

For grades 4–6, you might want to include: tundra, taiga, deciduous forest, grassland, desert, ocean, and tropical rain forest.

PRODUCER PRODUCER

POLLUTION POLLUTION

SECONDARY CONSUMER

SECONDARY CONSUMER

PRIMARY CONSUMER

PRIMARY CONSUMER

SCAVENGER
SCAVENGER
DECOMPOSER
DECOMPOSER

THIRD ORDER
CONSUMER

THIRD ORDER
CONSUMER

In grades 7–8, other biomes might be included, such as fresh water lake, salt marsh, tropical savannah, alpine tundra, or tropical monsoon. This would be a great time to check with the social studies teachers and have the students work on a biome of whatever area they are studying in that class.

Consider creating sets of cards for other biomes. Suggestions include:

> the freshwater stream biome
> the ocean biome
> the desert biome
> the grassland biome
> the tundra biome
> the tropical rainforest biome
> the mountain biome

◼◼◼ AWESOME CRITTERS ◼◼◼

INTRODUCTION

In search of a unit that is hands-on, exciting and stimulates student creativity? If you are looking to study animals that children love to research—and involve the whole class— as well as concretely demonstrate the inter-dependence of all living things, this one is for you.

OVERVIEW

Awesome critters involves students in surveying their parents, siblings, neighbors and friends. After the ten most feared creatures have been identified by the survey, students are then assigned the task of finding out as much as possible about one of the animals. Then the fun begins! They must create a campaign to save their animal. Signs, buttons, songs, poems, skits, bulletin boards, and anything else can be used to help save the dreaded animals. The grande finale comes when the judges listen to the reasons in the final presentations that the students put together to persuade the world of the great worth of that species. The judges evaluate each animal group according to the accuracy of the oral report, as well as the amount of effort students have put into the reports, posters, and other aspects of the campaign.

PROCEDURE

First Lesson

1. As a class discussion, students describe creatures of which they are afraid. Try to find out reasons WHY they fear that particular creature. Lists can be recorded on the blackboard, or on an overhead transparency.

2. After the list is relatively long, discuss how a scientist would find out which creatures are most feared by people. One way to find out which creatures other people fear is to ask them. Scientists use a tool called a survey to find out what people think about a certain subject. The students might create a survey to find out which creature the people in the area fear the most.

3. Set up guidelines so that all of the surveys are conducted using the same rules. Allow the students to come up with the rules and parameters for the survey, but make sure that they include the following:

   A person may be surveyed only once.

   They must give the name of a creature which is real, not including humans.

   Each student survey should have a minimum of 10 people. The more responses, the better!

   Survey respondents should not have any examples of answers from other people, nor should they be allowed to see the survey before giving a response.

4. Allow the students a few days to conduct their surveys.

Second Lesson

1. On the day that the surveys are due, have the students tally the responses for each creature mentioned on their own survey. For example: Sharks-6, Leeches-1, Elephants-2, etc.

2. Have one student name one animal on his/her list. Then ask the other students to count the number of responses that they have for the same animal.
   Add all of the responses from everyone's survey for the same creature. (A great "speedy addition" activity!)
   List the name of the creature on the board, and write the total number of responses for it after its name.
   Continue in similar manner until all responses have been counted and reported.

3. Next, ask the class to determine the top ten feared animals according to the surveys. All they need to do is to find the ten animals that have the highest numbers.
   Put the animals in order, the highest number first.

Make sure to have one of the students act as a recorder to copy the results of the class survey.

Post the list for the students and survey respondents to see.

Third Lesson

1. Before class begins, make one copy of the AWESOME CRITTERS information package for each student (see the sheets at the end of this section). Fill in the blank space with the name of one of the top ten dreaded creatures.

2. Give each student his/her AWESOME CRITTERS information package. Note that each student has his/her name already on the sheet, and that the creature that they will research is already filled in.

3. Read the sheets with the class and answer any questions that they have about how they are to proceed.

4. Determine the due date for the project. Allow at least two weeks for research, posters, plays, skits, buttons, testimonials, videos, and whatever else the students feel that they need to convince the judges of their creature's great value.

5. At this point, the teacher should contact the judges so that they can set up their schedules. The number of judges should be somewhere between 2 and 4. If too many more are involved, it gets to be too difficult to come to a consensus.

6. If possible, take the students to the library so they can begin their research immediately. Arrange for the students to have access to library materials throughout the project.

7. Each student should have a page or two of research notes before he/she is allowed to begin planning other aspects of the presentation with members of the group.

8. Once all members of a group have the required 1 or 2 pages of research notes, allow students to work on projects together, as long as they are the same type of creature.

   Remind students that each group of animals will be pleading their case together, so it is best to discuss what they are planning to present to avoid redundancy should they elect NOT to work together as a group. Check each student's progress as they work on the projects.

   Encourage students who are in need of support, but try to keep your ideas and opinions to yourself. Let it be each student's own project, not an imitation of your good ideas!

Judging and Evaluation

The judges should have the JUDGE'S EVALUATION SHEET and NOTES TO JUDGES (see the end of this activity) a few days before the actual judging is to take place so they can become familiar with the criteria for judging. It is helpful if you can offer each judge a clipboard and pencil for note-taking purposes, as well as multiple copies of the JUDGE'S EVALUATION SHEET. The judges will be announcing their decisions after all of the presentations have been completed. Notes help them to remember why they decided as they did.

It takes about three 40-minute periods to get through 10 presentations. It is helpful if the same judges can be available each day. Judges might be principals, assistant principals, teachers with a planning period while you are doing the presentations, guidance counselors, aides, or older students who have a study hall or free time during your class time period.

A few days before judging, post a list of which groups will go first, second, and so on. This allows the students to better gauge their time, and, if special perishable props are needed, arrangements can be made.

Invite parents to observe the proceedings, but try not to include them as judges. It is very difficult for both the child and the parent.

Allow students a certain amount of time to set up for their presentation. Five minutes is the most time that they should need. While they are setting up, it is helpful for the audience to review the presentation that they just saw. Take care that it is not an evaluation of the presentation. The review should be a restatement of what the audience thought the main points of the presentation were.

A class discussion of the whole project is helpful the day after the project is completed. It allows the teacher to listen to the students and therefore modify the activity if necessary. It also enables the students to gain some insight into the reasons for the project.

Some of the things that the students have created have been a great deal of fun. One group of spiders all wore black, and had black, cut-off paper bags on their heads with eight blue eyes glued to the bags. We could still see their mouths, but not their eyes and noses. As they talked about the wonders of spiders, they were spinning webs of string. As we watched them, the illusion became convincing! They truly looked like the spiders they were describing. Needless to say, they were selected to survive.

Another group, this time sharks, pleaded their case using tried and true methods; they called it SHARK AID. They offered the audience the opportunity to receive absolutely free a "shark aid" mug with every pledge of over $100 to help save the sharks. (They claimed they would even take personal checks and major credit cards!) They discussed facts about sharks as commercial messages between testimonials and other segments, urging their classmates to contribute to the cause. And all they had to do was dial 1-800-SHARK-AID.

A bunch of bears once tried to bribe the judges by offering them honey, which they promised to supply for a month, since bee stings didn't bother bears (unless they were stung on the nose). In the room, unfortunately for the bears, were the bees. They put up a howl of protest at first, but when it came time for their presentation, they stated that they were actually providing the honey for the judges—the bears were simply the delivery boys!

Wolves have howled their songs, and giant bees, snakes and spiders have all tried to explain why they are important to the world. The dutiful judges have announced with great flourish which groups were convincing and therefore survived, and which groups succumbed due to lackluster technique, preparation, or whatever. The class discussion that is held the day after the presentation is a time for changing and rearranging so that the next time, the whole project works better. Students really do have good suggestions, if we take the time to listen! But most of all, students are aware of the important part many creatures play in our world, even creatures that some people fear.

Name_____ Date_____

SURVEY SHEET

NAME OF CREATURE	WHY DREADED?	SIGNATURE

Please remember that all creatures listed as "dreaded" must be real. Imaginary beasts may not be listed. People may not be listed as a dreaded creature. (Even though they can be the most scary creatures of all!)

Remember not to let the person you are surveying see the survey sheet until *AFTER* he/she has responded.

You MAY NOT record a response if that person has already been surveyed.

This survey is due on _____

INFORMATION PACKET

(Name)_____, YOU are now a

(Name of creature)_____. In order to survive, you must persuade the judges that you are valuable to the world. Begin a campaign to *convince* the judges of your great worth. Begin in the library: just *why* are you and your kind valuable? What would happen if you and your kind vanished? Would insect populations suddenly increase? Would rodents be able to eat more and more crops? Would flowers no longer be pollinated? Would animal populations no longer be kept in balance? You will create an oral report which details the importance of your kind, including what would happen to the world if you were to disappear. In the report, you must decide the following:

- Your physical characteristics (you may include drawings, photographs, magazine pictures, etc.)
- A description of your habitat and your behavior
- A food web (your predators and your prey)
- Your relationship to other animals and plants (hiding places, homes, food, etc.)
- A description of the effects on the food web if you are eliminated
- Just *why* you are dreaded, mistreated, threatened, endangered. Can you find old wives tales, legends, myths or other information which helps to point out the senseless fear of your kind?
- A listing of your merits and reasons why your kind should be allowed to survive. Remember to include all aspects of your importance.

But Don't Stop There!

Your campaign can include posters, poems, songs, stories and testimonials that help to convince everyone of your great worth to our world. These posters, poems, songs, stories and testimonials can be hung in the halls, in classrooms, in the cafeteria, etc., as long as you are responsible for them. If they fall, you must retape them. When the project is over, you must remove them. Any materials found on the floor will result in *that* species losing some points in the final evaluation.

You might want to create pins and buttons to wear. These can have slogans.

You may form alliances with others of your kind. *But* you must do your own research when you prepare your part of the oral report. Get together with others of your kind and map out your strategy for your presentation. If you wish, you may present your own research without any other members of the group, but please consider that the judges will not look kindly on redundancy (the same thing said over and over again.)

Each species will present their findings orally to the panel of judges. Each presentation should be somewhere from two to ten minutes in length. While presenting, you may dress as the species you represent. All of the same species will be together in front of the selectors during the presentation. Please remember that one of the things that the judges are looking for is a creative presentation. Let your imagination go wild...be adventurous...dare to be unique.... In other words, don't just get in front of the room and read a report to the class.

Presentations may be in any form:

   —Simple oral presentation

   —A short skit (if you do this, don't lose sight of the purpose of the skit.
     You want to convince the selectors of your many reasons why you are
     valuable.)

   —A commercial for your species

   —A slide show (this takes a great deal of preparation)

   —A video recording

   —Any other reasonable method of presentation

A few days before the presentations are due, a list will be posted which will announce the day and order in which the presentations will be made. This is done so that props, costumes, or whatever can be brought to school on the day of the presentation.

EVALUATION

The judges will be evaluating your species using the following criteria:

   ★ The creatures have described the effect on the food web if their
     species disappears (for example, increased rodent or insect popula-
     tion, no flowers, no food for other animals, and so on.)

★ The creatures show that they know how they eat, sleep, defend themselves, and know other aspects and information about their kind.

★ The creatures are well prepared.

★ The creatures present themselves in an organized and creative manner, and do not repeat the same information over and over again.

★ The creatures have attempted to persuade the world how important they are to the world, using posters, signs, poems, songs, etc.)

★ If this category is not included in the presentation, the creatures will automatically *NOT survive*.

In order to be survivors, the creatures need to have successfully met the criteria in at least four of the five categories listed.

The judges will announce the results when everyone has completed their presentations.

All signs, posters, banners, etc., must be removed by the end of the next school day. If posters only have one side written on, please store them for reuse or turn them in for others to use another time. Please do not discard anything that can be reused or recycled.

NOTES TO JUDGES

Judges: Using the checklist on the JUDGE'S EVALUATION SHEET, please evaluate each species as they present their oral reports. In order to be successful and survive, the creatures must have four of the five categories checked.

—If they do not have NUMBER ONE checked, they automatically do not survive.

—You will find it most helpful if you take notes while each group is presenting their information so that at the end of the presentations, you can pinpoint the good (and not so good) aspects of the presentations.

—At the end of all of the presentations, you will be the ones who announce to the students which creatures survived and which ones didn't. Please be prepared to do this with a flourish and flair, in other words, **ham it up**! Hold them in suspense while you review the groups' strengths and weaknesses, and then announce whether or not those creatures survived.

—Before you complete the evaluation sheet, please check the halls, cafeteria, and classrooms for signs, posters, banners, and other campaign materials. It is important for you to comment on some of the slogans and other materials created by each group.

THANK YOU, THANK YOU, THANK YOU! for helping to make this activity one that the students won't forget soon!

Name_____ Date_____

JUDGE'S EVALUATION SHEET

Section: _____

Name of
Critters: _____

Names of students in this group: _____

_____

_____

_____ 1. Students have described the effect on the food web if their species should disappear.

_____ 2. Students show that they know how they eat, sleep, defend themselves, and know other aspects and information about their kind.

_____ 3. The members of the group are well-prepared.

_____ 4. The group presents themselves in an organized and creative manner, with little or no redundant information.

_____ 5. The students have attempted to show how important they are to the world through posters, signs, poems, songs, testimonials, etc.

NOTES:

section II
WONDERS OF THE GREEN WORLD

WILDFLOWER MYSTERIES

INTRODUCTION

Wildflowers can be useful to the classroom science teacher in many ways. When taking a class outside for an excursion, it is helpful to focus the class's attention on some of the amazing wildflowers that students have always walked past and never known about.

OVERVIEW

Students try to discover the identity of the mystery plants described on file cards.

NOTE: The plants described can be found in the fall in the northeast United States. If the plants cannot be found on your school site, find substitute plants and create new cards.

PROCEDURE

1. Duplicate the mystery card pages. Make one set of cards for each group. Laminate the cards if you wish to reuse them. Try to find a field guide to flowers for each group.

2. If you can enlist the help of another teacher, an aide, a parent or some other responsible adult, the activity will be greatly benefitted. That other person can be the one who verifies the answers for each group, allowing you to make sure that the groups who need help receive it. Also, make sure that all of the plants described by the cards are found within the boundaries that you have set.

3. Divide the class so that three or four students are in each group.

4. Announce to the class that some of the great mysteries of the plant world are found on the cards that they are about to use. The members of the group must work together to attempt to discover the identity of the plant on the card.

5. When the group thinks that it has found the identities of all of the plants described on the cards, the answers must be verified by the teacher. All guesses must be recorded on the OFFICIAL ANSWER FORM and all questions on the form must be completed before submitting the answers for verification.

6. Discuss the boundaries for the activity. Stress that groups may not wander past the boundaries. Suggest that the groups cooperate and work as harmoniously as possible.

7. Find a central point within the set boundaries, and announce that this is plant **mystery central headquarters**. All groups must report to this place to check the accuracy of their responses.

8. When the allocated time is up, gather the class and discuss the correct answers for each of the mystery cards.

MYSTERY PLANT NUMBER ONE

This plant is really a gas! Honestly! In its vigorous attempt to survive, it gives off an ethylene gas to kill its neighboring plants.

It was originally brought to North America as a food for bees.

Its name in French means "tooth of the lion."

The root of this plant can be dried and used as a coffee substitute, and the young leaves can be used as salad greens.

The blossoms can be picked and added to fritters…and those fritters taste delicious! The blossoms can also be used for making wine.

© 1990 by The Center for Applied Research in Education

MYSTERY PLANT NUMBER TWO

This plant can be found all around the world.

The leaves were used by the Indians to line their moccasins to make them feel more comfortable, to keep out the cold, and to help prevent fungus infections. The Native Americans showed the colonists, and they also lined their shoes with the leaves.

The Greeks soaked the blossoms of the plant in olive oil and used the resulting oil in cuts to prevent infections. They also wrapped their figs in the fuzzy leaves. They found that the figs that were wrapped up didn't rot as quickly as those that weren't.

Revolutionary War soldiers used the leaves to cover wounds when they were short on bandages. The side benefit of using the leaves for this pupose was that the wounds were less apt to become infected.

Native Americans also used the long stem for torches in ceremonies. They dried the stalk, and dipped it in melted fat, and then lit it. It lasted for quite a long time.

The plant has leaves that are soft and fuzzy the first year. The second year is when the long tall stalk appears.

MYSTERY PLANT NUMBER THREE

This plant has sap that gives it its name.

It is one of the few places where a monarch butterfly will lay its eggs because the monarch caterpillar usually only eats this plant. (Which makes the monarch caterpillar and the butterfly poison if any bird or other predator eats it!)

It has leaves that are opposite each other as they grow on the stem.

MYSTERY PLANT NUMBER FOUR

This plant looks like a small tree.

It is sometimes called the "Indian Lemonade Tree".

It has a relative that will cause you to break out in an awful rash that itches.

In late winter, Native Americans hollowed out the stems and used them as tubes for collecting maple sap.

Native Americans sometimes hollowed out the stems and used them as flutes.

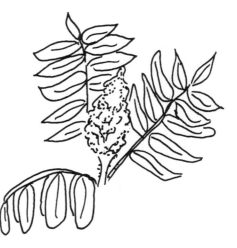

MYSTERY PLANT NUMBER FIVE

This plant is found growing in moist areas. Usually anywhere that poison ivy grows, it grows too! It is a good thing too, because it is an antidote plant for poison ivy. Should you accidentally touch poison ivy, and you quickly rub the juice of this plant on that spot, you won't develop the itchy rash you normally get with poison ivy.

If you hold the leaf of this plant underwater, it appears to turn silver. That's why one name for it is the "Aluminum Plant". (No, you can't use that as the correct name!)

The seeds are amazing! If you touch a ripe seed pod, it explodes!

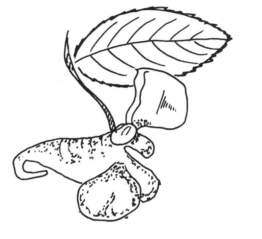

MYSTERY PLANT NUMBER SIX

This plant grows to be very large. It loses its leaves in the winter and grows back new ones in the spring.

The plant produces food that is enjoyed by bluejays, chipmunks, and sometimes even people!

In order for people to be able to use this plant's seeds as food, they need to boil it in water for several hours, changing the water every time the water turns yellow. When the water no longer turns yellow, the food should be dried in a slow oven. When dry, it is ground into coarse bits. After the preparation, this food can be used instead of flour.

Many other plants and animals live near this plant. It is a favorite of the gypsy moth.

MYSTERY PLANT NUMBER SEVEN

This plant is one of the first to become green in the spring.

Its bulbs were used by the Indians for food and flavoring.

The juice was used to open the nostrils during colds, and the juice was mixed with honey for asthma and coughs.

The juice was also used as an insect repellent.

Herb doctors applied the sliced bulb to the soles of the feet of people who had a fever, since the herb doctors thought that the hot taste would remove hot (fever) from the body.

MYSTERY PLANT NUMBER EIGHT

This plant is a native of the Mediterranean Sea.

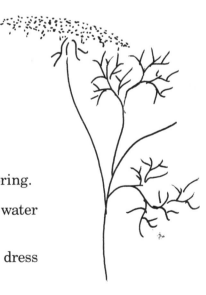

It is mentioned in 500 B.C. by the Greeks.

It is the wild version of the cultivated carrot.

In Europe many years ago, it was used as a cure for threadworms.

The reddish juice is used as a natural food coloring.

Mohican Indians steeped the blossoms in hot water and drank the juice as a cure for diabetes.

Its common name comes from the favorite dress decorations of one of the monarchs of England.

© 1990 by The Center for Applied Research in Education

9. ANSWERS TO THE MYSTERY PLANTS:

Plant number one   – dandelion
Plant number two   – great mullein
Plant number three – milkweed
Plant number four   – staghorn sumac
Plant number five   – jewelweed
Plant number six   – white oak
Plant number seven – wild onion
Plant number eight – Queen Anne's lace

10. After discussion, take the class back to each plant. Have students volunteer to name the plant and describe its uses.

11. If possible, have each group sketch one of the plants. Mount the sketches on a bulletin board with the mystery plant descriptions under each sketch. Label each with their common name as well as the Latin name.

OFFICIAL ANSWER FORM

GREAT PLANT MYSTERIES

Date:_____

Investigators:_____

_____

_____

_____

Plant Number One

We think that this is a _____

The reasons why we think so are:

_____

_____

_____

_____

_____

Plant Number Two

We think that this is a _____

The reasons why we think so are:

_____

_____

_____

_____

_____

Plant Number Three

We think that this is a _____

The reasons why we think so are:

_____

_____

_____

_____

_____

Plant Number Four

We think that this is a _____

The reasons why we think so are:

_____

_____

_____

_____

_____

Plant Number Five

We think that this is a _____

The reasons why we think so are:

_____

_____

_____

_____

_____

Plant Number Six

We think that this is a _____

The reasons why we think so are:

_____

_____

_____

_____

_____

Plant Number Seven

We think that this is a _____

The reasons why we think so are:

_____

_____

_____

_____

_____

Plant Number Eight

We think that this is a _____

The reasons why we think so are:

_____

_____

_____

_____

_____

For which plants could you create a mystery card?

_____

_____

_____

What hints would you include?

_____

_____

_____

_____

_____

_____

_____

■ USING WHAT YOU HAVE...VIOLETS! ■

INTRODUCTION

An infusion made from common violets can be used for many purposes. To make the infusion here's what to do:

1. Pick two cups of violet flowers. Only pick the purple flower.
   You should explain to the class that when you pick the violet flowers, you are not preventing the plant from multiplying. Common Blue Violets spread by their root systems as well as the explosive pods that send seeds scattering in many directions. The pods look like whitish unopened flowers, found near to the ground.

2. Place the flowers in a heat-proof container and (carefully, with adult supervision) add two cups of boiling water to the blossoms.

3. Allow the mixture to stand for 24 hours.

4. Strain the flowers from the juice and discard the flowers in the compost heap.
   A violet flower infusion can be used for a variety of purposes. For instance, the class can use it to test for acids and bases. It is an indicator!

A Violet Juice Indicator!

1. Using the recipe, make the violet infusion.

2. Divide the class into small working groups. Give each group some of the violet infusion.

3. Have them add some lemon juice to one small jar of the mixture and some cleanser to another jar of the violet juice.

4. Ask the class to report their findings.

5. Allow class discussion to find that the juice is an indicator just as litmus paper and pH paper are indicators.
   Red cabbage can also be used as an indicator. Simply substitute grated red cabbage for the violet flowers in the recipe above.
   When doing a lesson on indicators, why not allow the class to test various substances to determine whether each is an indicator or not?

VIOLET JELLY

INTRODUCTION

Another use for violet juice is to make violet jelly! It is really easy to make, tastes great and looks wonderful!

OVERVIEW

Using the recipe, students create the jelly, and then discuss the reasons for recipes, and how scientists use those recipes to pass information from generation to generation.

A NOTE OF CAUTION: Do not make jelly from violets that have had any lawn chemicals sprayed on them. Fertilizer, weed killer, or insecticides are things we don't want in our bodies. Make sure that your violet supply is untainted, and if you can't be sure, don't use them. It's okay to use tainted violets for the indicator lesson, but not for jelly!

PROCEDURE

Violet Jelly

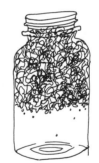

    2 CUPS OF VIOLET BLOSSOMS
    2 CUPS OF BOILING WATER
    2 CUPS SUGAR
    2 TABLESPOONS LEMON JUICE
    1 PACKAGE OF POWDERED PECTIN

Note: Make sure there is adult supervision whenever students are working with boiling water.

1. Place the violet flowers in a heat resistant container, and add the 2 cups of boiling water. Let stand for 24 hours.
2. Strain out the flowers and discard them. (Good compost material!)
3. Place the violet juice in a pan, add the lemon juice, and bring the mixture to a boil. Meanwhile, mix the packaged pectin with the sugar.
4. When the violet juice is boiling, add the sugar/pectin mixture. Stir constantly to keep the sugar from burning.
5. When the mixture boils so that it cannot be stirred down, begin to time the boiling for one minute.
6. After the minute, remove the pan from the fire, and skim the foam from the top of the jelly.

7. Pour into clean jelly jars and process in boiling water for five minutes.

8. Have the students make fancy labels for the jelly. The label should indicate the type of jelly, and the date the jelly was made.

When the jelly making is completed, discuss the reasons for using the recipe. Ask the class whether scientists use recipes for making things other than food? Why is it important for the recipe to be followed exactly? Is there a "recipe" for things such as steel? Can the class find out what that "recipe" is?

What other unusual "recipes" can the class find?

RESOURCES

To find more information about plants, the following books might be of value:

Gibbons, Euell. *Stalking the Healthful Herbs*. New York: David McKay Co. Inc., 1966.

> The book contains a wealth of information about how many wild plants can be used by people.

Lust, John. *The Herb Book*. New York: Bantam Books, 1974.

> This book has incredible amounts of information about the legends, medicinal uses, and household uses for wild plants found commonly throughout North America.

Peterson, Lee Allan. *A Field Guide to Wild and Edible Plants*. Boston: Houghton Mifflin Company, 1977.

> A great source for students to use when attempting to identify wildflowers. The uses for the plants give the reader a sense of the history of the plants.

Peterson, Roger Tory and McKenny, Margaret. *A Field Guide to Wildflowers*. Boston: Houghton Mifflin Company, 1968.

> A good source for plant identification, but very little background or plant use information is included.

Russell, Helen Ross. *Foraging for Dinner.* New York: Thomas Nelson, Inc., 1975.

> A great guide to wild edibles and how to prepare them.

Wilkins, Marne. *The Long Ago Lake*. San Francisco: Sierra Club Books, 1978.

> A great guide for plant uses as well as a gentle philosophy for being outdoors with children. Filled with stories and anecdotes that provide insight to the world outdoors.

UNDERSTANDING TREES

INTRODUCTION

This unit culminates in a simulation of the complex forces that are involved as trees make food. The teacher is the director and the children are the actors; they won't soon forget how a tree works after this activity. They will need a basic understanding of chemical formulas, atoms, molecules, and the elements hydrogen, oxygen and carbon to understand the Tree Simulation. They'll also need to know about the oxygen-carbon dioxide cycle. If your students aren't already familiar with these concepts, the lessons leading up to the TREE SIMULATION activity should prepare them adequately. Or, you can use the lessons as a review or skip right to the simulation itself.

The Chemistry of Trees: Background

1. Using class discussion, develop the following definitions with the class. As the definitions are worked out, ask different members of the class to record the definitions on the board. Use colored chalk! The kids love it, and the whole vocabulary lesson seems less dull and dreary! They can record definitions on the TREE CHEMISTRY: BACKGROUND VOCABULARY worksheet.

atom	hydrogen
molecule	carbon
element	carbon dioxide (CO_2)
compound	water (H_2O)
oxygen	simple sugar ($C_6H_{12}O_6$)
	chemical formulas

2. In some manner, teach the class to decipher chemical formulas and symbols for the elements carbon, oxygen and hydrogen.

   NOTE: A logical way to proceed is to introduce the formula for water first, then the formula for simple sugar. Next, use carbon dioxide's formula to determine whether the class truly understands.

TREE CHEMISTRY: BACKGROUND VOCABULARY

Use the spaces below to record information about the chemistry of trees.

1. atom _____

_____

2. molecule _____

_____

3. element _____

_____

4. compound _____

_____

5. oxygen _____

_____

6. hydrogen _____

_____

7. carbon _____

_____

8. carbon dioxide (CO_2) _____

_____

9. water (H_2O) _____

_____

10. simple sugar ($C_6H_{12}O_6$) _____

_____

11. chemical formulas _____

_____

_____

EVERYTHING YOU'VE NEVER ASKED ABOUT TREES

Get the kids curious about trees and how they work as you introduce the Tree Simulation.

PROCEDURE

1. Prepare a box with supplies such as:
     —pencils

     —clipboards (NO CLIPBOARDS? See the "OUTDOORS" section, Water Equipment, for making clipboards!)

     —hand lenses, (Inexpensive, effective plastic ones cost under one dollar, and kids love to look at things using hand lenses!)

     —paper, for notes, sketches, and ideas to be discussed when the groups have completed the questions.

2. Divide the class into small working groups and take them outside so that the class can observe a real tree.

3. When you arrive at the outdoor site where the class is to make their observations, hand each group an envelope that has the questions sealed inside (See "Questions About Trees"). The questions require the class to begin thinking about how trees work. The class will be fascinated if you take a little bit more time to find unusual envelopes. Varied colors, wild stickers, and other decorations make the whole lesson more festive. Glittery envelopes and other decorative touches make the class feel that they are on an adventure, not doing a school assignment. Use the magic! It really helps to keep the kids interested.

4. After each group has had a chance to read the questions inside the envelope, gather the groups and have them sit in a rough circle on carpet squares. Discuss the directions at the top of the page, so that everyone understands that they are to answer the questions using their best guess, and that if they don't know the answers, it is okay to make up answers. The answers do have to be reasonable, though.

5. Allow the groups enough time to work on formulating good answers to the questions. As they work, circulate among the groups encouraging answers. If this is the first time kids are asked to come up with theories about whether or not trees do anything beside sit in the forest, it might be difficult for many students to go past their original mindset. So, you need to encourage, cajole, and support the groups as they formulate their hypotheses.

6. After a reasonable amount of time, allow each group to present their answers to the questions. Make sure that you reward all groups' answers with your positive comments and make sure that all of the class is focusing on the ideas presented by each group.

QUESTIONS ABOUT TREES

Please answer these questions completely. If you don't know an answer...that's great! Because you will then have the chance to make up your own hypothesis. Some of the best discoveries that scientists have made, have been as a result of question-answering just like you are about to do. Don't worry about being wrong, with these questions it is most important that you have good reasons to support your answers, you don't have to be correct. Good Luck!

1. Why do trees have bark?

2. What happens inside of a tree? Do trees have hearts and lungs and stomachs as we do? If so, what do they look like? If not, what do they have?

3. Do trees eat? If so, what do they eat? If not, how do they survive?

4. Why do some trees lose their leaves and some keep their leaves (needles) all year round?

5. What do trees do for a forest?

A Silent Contest!

If some groups finish ahead of others, you might ask that group to list all of the things they find on/near one tree. Anything that they can't name, can be sketched. You can make it a "silent contest." Only when each group is finished with the task at hand, do they find out that there is a "silent contest"—in this case, to see which group can list the greatest number of things found under/around/near a tree. If you do have "silent contests" make sure that the results of the winning group's work is either discussed or posted on a bulletin board, so the group gets the necessary recognition for their efforts.

Be sure not to tell the class about the silent contest in advance, to prevent a group from rushing through their regular work to get to the contest. If the groups don't know about it ahead of time, they will work on the first assignment until they are done.

The Oxygen-Carbon Dioxide Cycle

On the day of the activity, it is important to be animated as you present this lesson. Students remember the fun of the day, as well as how the tree works.

1. Discuss the oxygen-carbon dioxide cycle with the class. One of the fun ways to do this is to have the class pantomime the cycle. Divide the class in half. Tell the first half of the class that they are plants. Have them stretch to the sunlight, feel the breezes that bring them rain so they can flourish. The air also brings the plants one of the essentials so that they can produce food....CARBON DIOXIDE! Have the class make a pulling-in motion to show that the plants take in CO_2. Then explain that the plants use the CO_2 to make food, and one of the waste products is oxygen. O_2 is used by the animals!

2. Indicate to the other side of the class that they are the animals. Tell them that animals run around and do lots of neat stuff, and one thing that all animals need to do is breathe O_2. Have the class breathe in deeply as their motion, and when the animals exhale, one of the by-products is CO_2! As the students exhale, have them direct the exhaled CO_2 towards the plants. The plants then take in the CO_2 (use the gathering motion) and produce O_2, the plants should direct the O_2 toward the animals. Have the actions repeated a few times so that the children have a chance to practice the cycle.

TREE SIMULATION

OVERVIEW

In the Tree Simulation, the class becomes a working tree complete with trunk, roots, leaves, xylem, and phloem. As you talk your way through the simulation, the students discover the things a tree needs to make food, what that food really is, which living things rely on trees, as well as the effect those things have on the tree. There is a bit of preparation of materials that must be done prior to the activity, but once everything has been made, it can be stored for use again next year. This is an effective simulation that actively involves everyone in the class. Note: be sure to read·it through completely before conducting it.

MATERIALS NEEDED

100 red 1″ construction paper circles (carbon atoms)

100 blue 1″ construction paper circles (hydrogen atoms)

200 green 1″ construction paper circles (oxygen atoms)

2 boxes of paperclips

4 green signs labeled "chlorophyl"

1 sun/moon sign

1 sign labeled "air"

2 signs labeled "roots"

4 signs labeled "animals"

2 small pieces of cardboard (aprox 2″ × 4″) folded in half to protect the hands of the "tree."

2 4″ × 8″ pieces of felt, folded in half, stapled along the side edges, with 10 feet of yarn or string stapled to one side. The felt pieces should be labeled on both sides. One felt pocket is labeled "xylem," the other "phloem."

1 thin cross section of a tree (either real or made of paper)

1 large ball

PROCEDURE

1. Divide the circles between two open boxes: place 100 red and 100 green circles in one box and 100 blue and 100 green circles in the other. Place one box of paperclips in each box.

2. Select a volunteer and ask the student to stand on top of a sturdy table that you have placed in front of the classroom. Ask that student to stand with his/her arms stretched overhead like the branches of a tree.

3. Find four volunteers to act as the leaves of the tree. Each leaf should stand (carefully!) on one of the chairs that you have placed around the table. Discuss the function of leaves with the class. They should be able to deduce that one of the functions of a leaf is to make the food for the tree. Tell the class that the leaves have a special chemical to make their food which is called chlorophyl. Hang a sign labeled "chlorophyl" on each of the leaves.

4. Select another volunteer and place the large cutout of the sun and the moon over that person's head. The sun should hang on the front of the person, the moon hangs on the person's back. Have the sun practice being day and night by facing the class (day) and then turning around (night).

5. Explain that the tree makes food using three things and energy from the sun.

Chlorophyl is one of the things that the tree needs...elicit answers from the class as to what they think those other two things might be.

6. Since you just did the oxygen cycle, the class should come up with the answer, carbon dioxide. The carbon dioxide is taken in through openings on the bottom of the leaves called *stomata*. These openings are the gateways allowing carbon dioxide into the leaf, and the exit by which oxygen (and water vapor) is given off.

7. Ask one student to wear the label "air." Then appoint a group of four students and ask them to wear labels that announce them as animals. Give this group a box filled with red and green construction paper circles and a box of paper clips. Tell the animals that they have the job of breathing. But since this is a graphic demonstration, they need to show us the CO_2 they give off. So they must put together molecules of CO_2. Hang up a sign that indicates which atoms each color represents (green—oxygen, red—carbon, blue—hydrogen) and how to paperclip them together to form molecules.

The animals need to make molecules of CO_2 and give them to the air.

The air will carry the CO_2 to the leaves on the tree.

(Demonstrate how to make a molecule, by taking one carbon atom, two oxygen atoms, and clipping them together with a paperclip.)

8. Quickly review the items that have already been discussed, that trees need to make food. (Chlorophyl, CO_2, and sunlight)

9. Find two students to sit under the table. Give them each a sign that says "roots," a box of red and blue circles and paper clips. Now we can discuss the last ingredients: water and minerals!

   Ask the class how water and minerals get to the leaves. Allow for answers. Either confirm or explain (depending on the answers that you get) that the water and minerals get to the leaves from the earth through a layer of cells called the xylem. The xylem goes all around the tree trunk and brings water and minerals up from the soil.

   If you have a cross section of a tree available, show the class the thin band where the xylem layer is located. If you can't get your hands on a real "tree cookie," make one from cardboard or paper.

10. To show that the xylem sends water and minerals to the leaves, take the felt pocket labeled xylem, and place it on the floor by the roots. Bring the string attached to the pocket up to the tree's upstretched hands. (Be sure to place a piece of cardboard or plastic on the hand before placing the string, so the string doesn't cut into the person's hand.)

11. Have one of the roots gather a molecule of water from the box of hydrogen and oxygen atoms. Place the molecule in the felt pocket, and have the root pull up the water molecule.

12. Point out that all of the necessary items are in place for the leaves to make food.

    —Ask the "air" person to bring a carbon dioxide molecule to the leaf, and tell that person to keep on going back and forth to bring CO_2 molecules to the leaves.

    —Request that the roots keep gathering water molecules and sending them up to the leaves.

    —Now tell the leaves that they can use these molecules to make their food, $C_6H_{12}O_6$! Ask the class if anyone remembers what that is the formula of? Of course, it's sugar.

13. Have the leaves work together to make sugar molecules from the CO_2 and H_2O molecules. After a few have been made, ask the leaves what they are going to do with them. They should respond that they will feed the tree.

14. When the leaves have made about ten sugar molecules, announce that they are very efficient leaves. They have made more food than the tree needs for right now. Ask the class what the tree might do with extra food? When someone finally says "store it in the roots," bring out the other felt pocket labeled phloem.

    Tell the class that the phloem, like the xylem, is a layer of cells that go all around the tree. The phloem takes extra sugar and stores it in the tree's roots for the future needs of the tree. Show the students the cross section of the tree again, and point out that the phloem layer is right next to the xylem layer.

    To keep the students from confusing the layers and their functions, you might remind the class that "the *phloem flows down.*"

15. Make sure that the class understands that the xylem *only* takes water and minerals up, and the phloem *only* takes sugar down.

16. Allow the action to continue for a few minutes so the rest of the class can watch the process. Every once in a while, ask the sun to turn to night so the leaves have to stop making food. (The animals and the air and the roots can keep on doing their thing; only the leaves have to stop.)

    —Depending on how sophisticated the class is, you might mention that a dark reaction is involved in the process of photosynthesis. It follows the more familiar light reaction.

    —Also, some trees are able to carry on photosynthesis during the night when there is a full moon!

17. Once the process gets moving smoothly, announce that the tree is an oak tree and it is a very successful oak. The oak has just turned 50 years old, and is ready to produce its first acorns!

18. Have four or five students stand near the chairs where the leaves are working (hanging around, so to speak.) Naturally, acorns entice squirrels and bluejays to come and live near the oak. Appoint a bluejay and a squirrel and allow them each to "take" an acorn.

19. Spiders and other insects live in the tree as well.
    Find three students who are willing to be spiders and insects you can appoint one student as the spider and the others as insects, and allow the spider to take one of the insects as prey.

20. There are also special wasps that come and plant their eggs inside the leaves of the tree. The leaf forms a gall, (a large swelling) which shelters and feeds the larva of the wasp until the larva becomes an adult wasp in the next spring. Have a wasp designee pretend to sting one of the leaves and give that leaf a large ball that he/she must hold as he/she makes food molecules.

21. Even the gypsy moth gets into the act! Appoint some seated students to be the gypsy moth larvae. Announce that the caterpillars eat one fourth of the leaves of our tree. (Ask the class to compute how many of the "leaves" the caterpillars may remove.) Allow the gypsy moth larvae to take away one of the leaves. But, because the roots have been storing the extra food, the tree can grow new leaves! Ask a seated student to be a leaf.

22. Depending on how many students you have and how long you want to continue, you may choose to have ants bring aphids to the tree to suck the juices from the leaves, and then send in the lady bugs to the rescue. (Lady bugs eat the aphids that the ants use as "cows." When the aphids are eaten, the ants go away.)

23. One day, a branch falls off, and a woodpecker finds a home in the hole left by the fallen branch. The woodpecker then eats some of the insects that are bothering the leaves and tree.

24. When each student has had at least one role, send everyone back to their seats. Make sure that you applaud their good work. "Clap for yourselves, you've done a good job" is a standard that works well.

25. Ask the class to review the process orally as a review and closing for the tree activity simulation.

EXTENSIONS

Discussion questions might include:

—When early settlers arrived in new lands, they needed to clear the forests to make fields. They removed the bark from the tree in a complete circle around the tree. A year later they would return to chop down the tree. Why did they do that?

—In the summertime, if you sit under a tree you are cooled by its shade. How else does the tree work to keep you cool?

It's Fall—Why Do the Leaves Turn Colors?

Sometime after you have done the tree simulation activity, you may wish to explain why leaves of deciduous trees turn colors in autumn.

1. Set up your tree again. You'll need the tree trunk (on the table), roots (under the table), and leaves (on the chairs around the tree trunk).

2. Have the roots send water to the leaves via the xylem. Explain that trees take gallons and gallons of water from the earth and put it in the air. The process is called transpiration. The water exits the tree by the stomata.

3. To begin the simulation, hand each of the "leaves" a piece of green construction paper with either brown, yellow or orange construction paper clipped to the other side. Put a sign in each of the tree trunk's hands that says "abscission layer." After the signs are in the tree's hands, ask the leaves to unclip the green and slowly let it slip away. The other colors are now readily seen.

As this action is taking place, explain to the class that as the summer turns to fall, the number of daylight hours decrease, a layer of special cells between the tree and the leaf begins to form. This is called the abscission layer. Eventually, this layer prevents the water from reaching the leaf. The leaf cannot produce food anymore, since it is missing one of the necessary ingredients…water! The chlorophyl begins to break down. As the chlorophyl fades away, other colors that were masked by the strong green of the chlorophyl can now be seen. The browns, yellows and oranges were always there!

Discussion questions that might follow can be where do the reds and purples come from? Have the class create their own questions. Have the students form research teams to find the answers to the questions that are formulated. Research teams can report back to the class when they have found the answers to their questions.

Good Books About Trees!

People of all ages like to listen as someone reads a story. Here are some great books about trees that you might want to read to the class:

Mabey, Richard. *Oak and Company*. New York: Greenwillow Books, 1983.

> *Oak and Company* tells about the life of an oak tree and the

plants and animals that rely on the tree. If at all possible, read this to the class while seated under an oak!

One of my most memorable experiences happened while I was doing just that. As I read, I could feel the class' attention shift. I looked over, and there was a chipmunk, sitting next to me, listening to the story. One student became so excited that she disturbed the chipmunk, and it scampered away. As I continued to read, once again I felt the students' focus shift, but this time, they were focused to an area above my head. The chipmunk had returned, to a safer spot!

When we returned to the classroom, a discussion developed as to why the chipmunk joined our group. Was it because it was curious? Did it like the sound of my reading? Did our presence indicate food, as perhaps people who were picnicking would? The debate was never settled, but we all felt that we were incredibly lucky to have had an animal voluntarily join our class.

Ernst, Kathryn. *Mr. Tamarin's Trees*. New York: Crown Publishers, 1976.

> This book is out of print, but you can get a copy through the inter-library loan service. It is really worth the trouble!

The story goes like this: Mr. Tamarin hates to rake the leaves in the fall, so despite Mrs. Tamarin's protests, he cuts down all of the trees. Without the trees, they have real problems. Not only does their house look ugly, but the winter winds aren't stopped by the trees, so their front door freezes shut. The spring rains aren't soaked up by the trees, so the yard turns to mud. The house is no longer cooled by the trees in the summer. They try to sell the house, but no one wants to buy it— without the trees. They decide to plant new trees, and after many years, the trees grow and Mr. Tamarin is as content as his wife.

The illustrations are wonderful! This story is one that can be read to audiences of all ages, and they love it!

Buscaglia, Leo. *The Fall of Freddie the Leaf.* New York: Holt, Rinehart, Winston, 1982.

> Freddie and his friends are leaves who live on a tree. The story takes us through the seasons, until autumn arrives and the leaves must let go of their tree. It is a story that describes all living things.

Bellamy, David. Illus. Jill Dow. *The Forest*. New York: Clarkson N. Potter, Inc./ Publishers, 1988.

> This beautifully illustrated book first describes the natural forest; then the forest is taken over by a company interested in creating an industrial forest. It points out that only a few animals can survive in a monoculture forest. The rest need to live elsewhere. It is a good way to introduce the concept of the need for diversity in our world.

■■■■■ PLANT A REAL HERB GARDEN ■■■■■

INTRODUCTION

Creating and caring for an herb garden at school is always a possibility for a class project. We created one for a space outside of the library doors.

OVERVIEW

The students research soil preparation, the histories and uses of various herbs, as well as traditional herb garden patterns. When the research is completed, the actual garden is created. The work is shared by all, with everyone taking a turn at digging, mixing, and planting. In that way, the garden belongs to everyone.

PROCEDURE

1. Secure permission from your administrator to create the garden.
2. START SMALL! Don't create a giant garden that is quickly out of control. We limited our garden to 25 square feet.
3. We invited guest speakers to discuss herbs with us, and visited local herb gardens. The local historical society maintains an herb garden and uses the herbs throughout the old fort that they maintain. The class really had a chance to see how important the herbs were to the settlers.
4. Have the class research soil preparation, and the histories and uses of herbs. Each student should investigate ten herb plants. Included in the research should be:

    historical uses

    legends

    modern uses

    physical characteristics

    soil needs

    animals and insects that are attracted by the flower of the herb.
5. Each student should select one plant that he/she wishes to present to the class as a potential plant for the herb garden.
6. After all the presentations have been made, each student votes for the ten plants which he or she feels should be in the garden. The top ten vote getters are the ones to be included.
7. When the plants have been selected, decide how to obtain the herbs.

Some can be obtained from friends who already have herbs in their gardens.

Some that are best started from seed can be ordered through seed catalogs.

Herbs that are best purchased already growing can be purchased from local garden supply stores.

8. After selecting the ten plants that will be included in the garden, all students make a design for the garden. Discuss the merits of each design.

—Is the design aesthetically pleasing?

—How easy will it be to maintain?

—Will the maintainance crew be able to mow around the garden?

—Can we weed the garden without stepping in it?

—Who will tend the garden in the summer?

—What will we do with the herbs once they are grown?

9. Have the class make a list of supplies that are needed, and decide who will make the purchases.

10. Prepare the soil and plant the garden. Water it frequently, unless there is frequent rain.

RESOURCES

Several books are wonderful sources of information:

Lust, John. *The Herb Book*. New York: Bantam Books, 1974.

> This book is an encyclopedia of plants. It discusses what plants look like, and how they are used. Included in uses are medicinal uses, dyes, spices, substitutes for coffee, herb teas, cosmetics, perfumes, and other uses. It contains a plant's history as well as the legends and lore of some of the herbs.

Morton, Julia. *Herbs and Spices*. New York: Golden Press, 1976.

> This is a good book for identifying herbs. It appears to be written with the student in mind. The herbs are illustrated, and labeled with their Latin name and common name. It describes where the plants originated and how the people used them, as well as the way the plant is used today.

The seed catalogs that are published by major nurseries are also good sources for discovering basic information about herbs. Information that can be found in the catalogs includes how tall plants grow, whether they are annual or perennial plants, what they look like, in which climates they will flourish and when they should be planted.

"THE HERB QUARTERLY," published in Newfane, Vermont 05345, is a delightful publication well worth the cost of the subscription. It will help the class to understand herbs and the traditions of herb gardens.

If you have lots of money, you may wish to purchase John Gerard's, *The Herbal*. It is published by Dover Press. It is the 1633rd version of the book which is considered one of the best when it comes to describing herbs. If you don't want to buy the book, perhaps your library has a copy. If they don't, remember that there's always the inter-library loan service.

A Wild Garden

If you don't want to plant herbs, you may wish to cultivate wild plants that can be used as food, dyes, or whatever. Some good books that will help the students to make good decisions are:

Brown, Tom Jr. *Tom Brown's Guide to Wild Edible and Medicinal Plants*. New York: Berkley Books, 1985.

Coon, Nelson. *Using Wild and Wayside Plants*. New York: Dover Press, 1980.

Densmore, Frances. *How Indians Use Wild Plants for Food, Medicine and Crafts*. New York: Dover Press, 1974.

Gibbons, Euell. *Stalking the Healthful Herbs*. New York: David McKay Co. Inc., 1966.

Peterson, Lee Allen. *A Field Guide to Edible Wild Plants*. Boston: Houghton Mifflin Co., 1977.

Russell, Helen Ross. *Foraging for Dinner*. Nashville: Thomas Nelson, Inc. Publishers, 1975.

HERB GARDEN PATTERNS

INTRODUCTION

Why not go one step farther with a plant growing project? When it is necessary to grow plants for science lessons or other reasons, why not use this quick, easy-to-do, problem solving activity? It keeps the class thinking, yet provides a source of fun and excitement as plants are grown for science experiments or other activities.

OVERVIEW

The class grows herbs for their science projects. The activity involves the manner in which the plant containers are arranged. This quick, simple, fun, observational activity keeps the class thinking.

PROCEDURE

Materials

- milk cartons from the students' lunches that have been washed and dried or the bottom of 2 liter soda bottles. (see water equipment)
- enough potting soil to fill each container ³/₄ full
- seeds

1. Obtain a seed catalog and decide which types of herbs the students wish to grow. Considerations might include plant size, plant use, ease of seed germination, as well as other factors.
2. Once the plants have been grown, display several pictures of traditional herb garden designs. Make sure that the location of the garden is labeled.
3. As a thinking skill type activity, while the class is out of the room, rearrange the plants to resemble, as closely as possible, one of the herb garden patterns.
4. When the class returns, ask them how the plants have been arranged. Students will suggest various patterns, and, one hopes, someone will discover a similarity to one of the herb gardens on display.
5. When no one else is listening, ask the student who correctly guessed the answer to arrange the herbs in a different pattern the next time the class is out of the room. That student might wish to recreate a different herb garden pattern, and he/she may wish to arrange the herbs using each plant's common name in alphabetical order, by potential plant height, or any other method. Provide assistance and technical help for the student as needed to insure the accuracy of the pattern.

6. Again, when the class returns, have the students reason out how the plants have been arranged. The correct guesser has the right to provide the next rearrangement, and so on.

TOMATO SKINS

INTRODUCTION

Use a tomato to have the class begin a study of molds, or to have the class begin a study of the function of skin. This is quick and easy...and the kids love it!

OVERVIEW

This activity focuses on the function of outer coverings on fruits and vegetables, and then turns to focus on the molds that attack the fruits and vegetables. Students set up their own experiments, predict the outcome of the experiment, and then verify the results.

PROCEDURE

1. Bring two tomatoes to class. Discuss the qualities of the skin of the tomato with the class.
2. Set up an experiment so that the skin of one of the tomatoes is intact, while the other skin is pierced in only one place.
3. Ask the class to predict what will happen. Will there be no change in either tomato? Will the one with the pierced place decay more quickly? If mold grows, what color will it be?
4. After a day or two, the changes in the pierced tomato will be evident. Discuss these changes with the class. Ask the class to speculate on where the mold came from.
5. Ask the students to create their own experiments. After they predict the outcomes, they should conduct the experiments and verify the results.

EXTENSIONS

1. Have the class look at the various molds under a microscope and draw the molds.
2. Have the class set up a "Mold Hall of Fame." Students research different types of mold and how those molds affect people. When the class has finished their research, they can display their findings on a bulletin board.
3. Use this lesson to kick off a study of human skin.

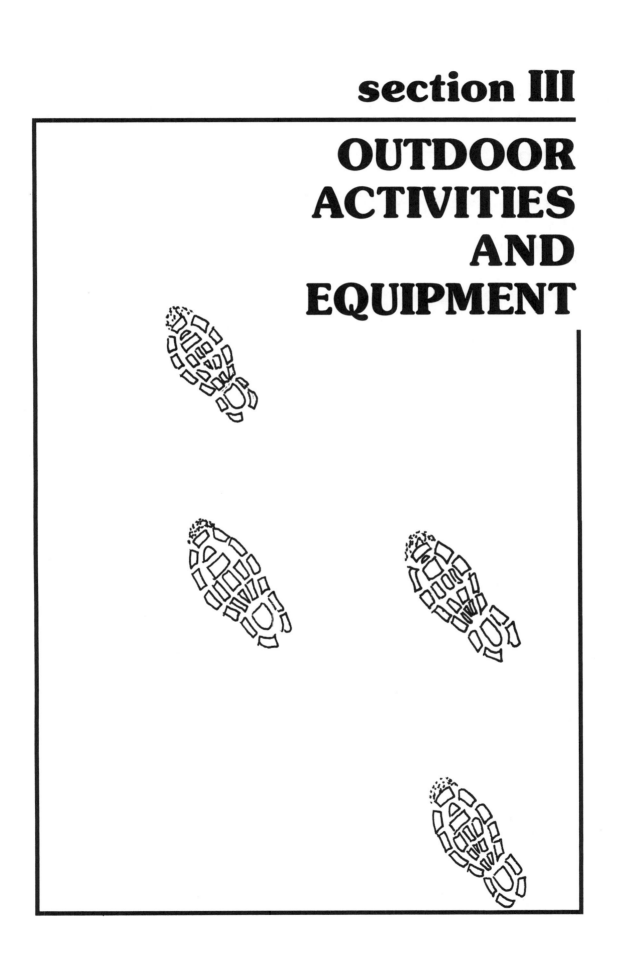

section III

OUTDOOR ACTIVITIES AND EQUIPMENT

■■■ TRACKING PEOPLE IN THE SNOW ■■■

INTRODUCTION

This is no ordinary drag and brag session on animal prints in the snow, this is a real tracking exercise where a few of the students act as the "animals," and small groups of students act as "research teams" in an attempt to track the animals to photograph them.

OVERVIEW

Students create snowshoes from recycled materials. The snowshoes have a distinct print and enable the researchers to track the "animal." As the activity progresses, the tracking becomes harder and harder since tracks begin to overlap one another!

PROCEDURE

Materials

—Photographs, drawings and casts of animal tracks

—Recycled materials of all sorts...plastic meat trays, empty plastic milk containers, cardboard boxes, juice cans, yogurt cups, plastic bags, and anything else that can be added to the assortment of materials.

—String, glue, fasteners, scissors, staplers, and other assorted fastening devices.

—One instant camera loaded with film for each group.

1. Distribute photographs or drawings of various animal tracks. Select tracks that students can readily recognize. Discuss the tracks that animals leave in the snow. Rabbits, mice, and deer are all animals that should be discussed. Don't forget to include chickadees, cardinals, hawks and others.

If casts of animal tracks are available, allow the class to examine them.

2. Announce to the class that they are about to create special snowshoe-type feet from recycled materials. They need to create a cover for each foot that will leave an unusual print for the researchers to follow. Each student will have the opportunity to act as the animal, and a few opportunities to act as trackers.

3. Allow enough time for each student to create his/her tracking feet. (This might be done a day or two prior to the actual tracking event.)

4. Divide the class into groups of 4 or 5 students who will be able to work together well. Each student will take a turn at being the animal that attempts to elude the researchers (the rest of the group).

5. Set the ground rules for the activity.

—Define the area that the students can be in. The larger the better, but make sure you have the ability to call them all in when necessary. One of those aerosol boat signal-makers is ideal. Just plug your ears before you sound it...it's LOUD!

—Discuss safety factors which must be considered at your site. Make sure that students do not cross busy roads, slide down ravines, or engage in any other treacherous activity. Safety first!

—The animal from each group is allowed a two minute head start before the rest of the group begins the pursuit.

—This is an activity of finesse. Once the researchers have located the animal, the animal gracefully allows his/her photo to be taken. They may not run away and continue to hide once they have been discovered.

—Animals should, on the other hand, try to be as tricky as possible. Print-making boot covers can be removed and slipped on backwards...hopping is allowed...so is swinging from branches or climbing trees. But once they are discovered, they should gracefully acknowledge the fact so that the next animal can have her/his turn.

—Should a group hopelessly lose its quarry, there must be a central point of return for the groups. There must also be a time limit for each animal.

6. Determine each animal's time limit by the total available time, allowing the last ten minutes for discussion of the activity, divided by the number of students per group.

7. Discussion might center around the following questions:

—Which were the easiest animals to track? Why?

—What tricks did some of the animals use?

—How did it feel to be a hunted animal?

—If you had the chance to redesign the snowshoes, how would you change your design?

—What were the most effective hunting techniques?

RESOURCES

The class might really enjoy this experience, and some of them might show an interest in tracking real animals. There are many good books that they can use. I have used the following books successfully with students:

Brown, Tom Jr. and Morgan, Brandt. *Tom Brown's Field Guide to Nature Observation and Tracking.* New York: Berkley Books, 1983.

Nestor, William P. *Into Winter.* Boston: Hougton Mifflin Company, 1982.

Stokes, Donald W. *A Guide to Nature in Winter.* Boston: Little, Brown and Company, 1976.

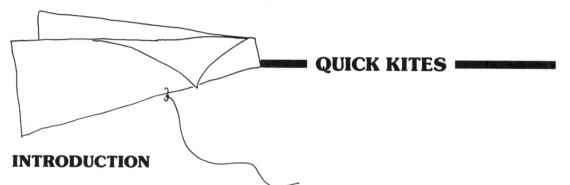

QUICK KITES

INTRODUCTION

Once, in the springtime, I wanted the class to create kites so that we could study the winds, how things fly, and have fun as we did it. So, I asked the class to create kites. It was a grueling project. Most of the students had little experience with creating kites, and their designs left much to be desired. The project took much more time than I had budgeted, and the resultant kites were less than satisfactory. I almost gave up on kites after that experience. I didn't really want the class to bring in store bought kites, and they didn't really have the skills to create their own.

Fortunately, I thought of a solution to my problem: paper kites! They are somewhat like paper airplanes, but they act like real kites. They are simple to construct, and the materials are readily available. They can be test flown indoors, and, best of all, they really work!

OVERVIEW

Paper kites are constructed in the classroom and tested outside to determine wind direction and wind speed. Kites can also open up discussions as to why things fly.

PROCEDURE

See the diagram for a visual!

1. Make an 8″ square from a piece of scrap paper.
2. Fold the paper in half, but only half way down.
3. Measuring from the top of the fold, make a mark at the 1½-inch point and the 3½-inch point.

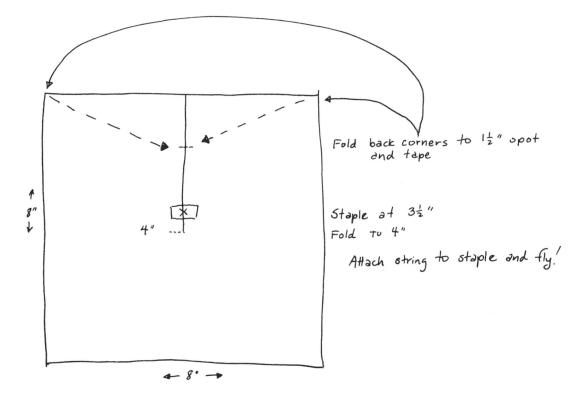

Fold back corners to $1\frac{1}{2}$" spot and tape

Staple at $3\frac{1}{2}$"
Fold to 4"

Attach string to staple and fly!

4. Open the paper so that the fold makes a tent on the table.
5. Take the top edges of the paper and tape them to the mark at the 1½-inch point.
6. To strengthen the 3½-inch point, put a piece of clear tape over the spot.
7. Put one staple at the 3½-inch point.
8. Attach the end of a spool of polyester thread to the staple.
9. Holding the spool, let out some string and walk quickly with the kite in tow. It will gracefully sail along behind you.

WATER EQUIPMENT

INTRODUCTION

Kids of all ages are fascinated by water. It doesn't matter whether the water is an ocean, lake, pond or puddle. People love to look at, be near, and, depending on the weather, be in the water. Take advantage of the interest inherent in water! When studying plants and animals, have the class study the plants and animals that live in the water too.

Equipment for water study can be either purchased or you can make your own. Naturally the home-made version won't be as fancy as the store bought equipment, but it will work.

OVERVIEW

Students will create equipment for studying the plants and animals found in puddles, ponds, streams, lakes, and rivers.

UNDERWATER VIEWING BOXES

funnel

Trying to look into the water can be a problem since light reflects on the surface of water. Using an underwater viewing box breaks the surface tension of the water and allows for better observation of the events that are taking place in the water.

PROCEDURE

underwater viewing box

Plastic 2-Liter Soda Bottle Version

1. Gather enough clear-sided 2-liter soda bottles for each viewer you need.
2. Soak the bottle in warm water to remove the label.
3. Remove the bottom cap from the bottle. It takes some pulling and prying. Sometimes it helps to keep the cap on the top of the bottle to provide firm support. (The bottom cap can be saved and used for planting seeds in another lesson.) Make sure that the bottom is rounded and smooth, so you can look through it. You have the wrong kind of bottle if it is lobed.
4. Using a sharp knife or scissors, cut the bottle so that the top is removed. (That top makes a great funnel for birdseed or whatever!) Make sure all safety precautions are observed and there is adult supervision of all cutting.
5. Use duct tape to tape the top edges so they aren't sharp anymore.

flower pot

The Better, More Expensive Model

You need some carpentry skills and equipment to create these. One source of labor if you don't have the necessary skills is the high school shop department or the vocational school building trades program.

1. Materials needed are plywood, plexiglass, caulking, and waterproof paint.
2. Cut four pieces of plywood and one piece of plexiglass so that each piece is 12 inches square. (Or you can make the box any size you wish.)
3. Using four pieces of plywood, make the sides of the box. Nail the sides together.
4. Attach a piece of plexiglass for the bottom of the box. Caulk around the inside joints to make the box waterproof.
5. Paint the outside of the box with waterproof paint.

Seining Net

Let the kids discover some of the animal life in a stream or pond by using a seining net.

1. You'll need two sturdy sticks, about as thick as broom handles, an old sheer curtain, some sinker weights, and some ping pong balls.
2. Using a heavy duty staple gun, attach the ends of the sheer curtain to the poles.
3. Sew the sinker weights to the bottom of the curtain, and attach the ping pong balls to the top edge of the curtain. (Use a large needle to poke a hole in the ping pong balls and use polyester thread to secure the balls to the net.)

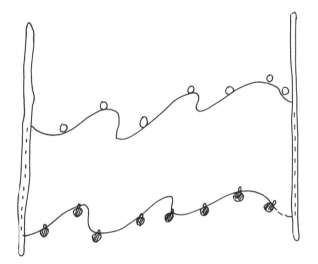

Hip Boots

We once tried to make homemade hip-wading boots by taping heavy-duty plastic garbage bags around kids' legs. (We used duct tape.) At first the garbage bags held up, but by the time the seining teams were done, the bags had worn through and the kids' legs were as wet as if they hadn't worn any bags.

If you do want to buy real hip-waders, please be careful. Hip boots work well, but if a student slips and falls in the water, the boot will fill up and sink. To demonstrate to the students how serious a water-filled boot can be, fill a hip wader with water, and let the students feel how heavy the boot is when filled. It is most certainly heavy enough to act like an anchor!

For this reason, we didn't even consider using chest-wading boots. In a fast stream, one slip can be a disaster for the novice chest boot wearer.

We finally did have the money to buy hip boots. To avoid potential problems, as a class we came up with the following safety rules for hip boot wearers:

1. Never attach hip boots to the belt of the wearer.
2. Before wading into the water, students should practice releasing the boot's buckle and getting it off quickly. (If a student cannot get a boot off in 45 seconds on land, that person should not put on the boots.)

3. All boot wearers should know how to swim.

4. The boot wearing team must plan where they are taking the seining net, and stick to that plan.

Dip Net

This net is used to catch animals that are visible in the water.

1. You'll need a wire coat hanger, a piece of an old sheer curtain, and needle and thread for this one!

2. Select the shape for the net. Cut net and sew it.

3. Bend the coat hanger and attach the net with needle and thread.

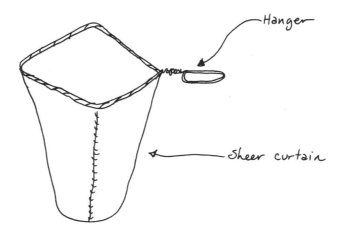

Collecting Boxes

Collecting boxes should be at the site where the class is studying the animals of the water. They are boxes half-filled with water from the stream. The boxes allow the students to observe the animals that have been collected with dip nets and seining nets. It also allows the animals to live as they are being observed.

When the day's study has ended, the animals can be safely returned to the river or stream.

Good collecting boxes are water tight, and light in color so that the class can easily see the animals that are swimming around in them.

We use the white enamel drawers from a discarded refrigerator. If you don't have an old refrigerator around, plastic tubs or any large container that will hold water is fine. Restaurants can be a good source of these.

Note: The class can watch as a dragonfly nymph darts around the box in its jet-propelled manner and it is a wonderful sight. But the dragonfly nymph is an aggressive insect, and it will eat almost anything that is in the collecting box with it, so try to keep them separate from other things that you wish to observe.

There are other insects that are aggressive as well, so it is always a good plan to have 3 or 4 collecting boxes to allow room for the different types of animals that might be found.

Clipboards

When outside with the class, it is difficult for the students to take notes and make drawings unless they have some sort of flat hard surface to lean on. Clipboards are great since they even provide a means by which the papers will stay with the board. If possible, try to get the school to purchase enough clipboards so that there is at least one clipboard for every two students.

If the budget is real tight, and there is no way that clipboards can be purchased, there are still ways to have good work surfaces.

One way is to find some discarded plywood, masonite or other type board. Ask the friendly shop teacher or vocational school folks to please cut the wood into 9″ x 12″ pieces. Sand any rough edges. Use two heavy duty rubber bands around the top and the bottom of the board to anchor the papers that the students are working on.

If you can't find plywood or masonite, you can try using cardboard. If you cut the cardboard into 9″ x 12″ pieces, and then hold three or four pieces of cardboard together with heavy duty rubber bands, it will work satisfactorily. The only problem is that they aren't waterproof, and if the kids press too hard, the cardboard will bend.

Observation Boxes

The clear plastic boxes in which some fast food restaurants serve their salads make wonderful observation boxes. The boxes can be used for aquatic insects or for terrestrial insects. To prepare the box, make holes in the top half of the container. An ice pick or any other round, sharp implement usually makes good, but small holes. Make lots and lots of holes so the air will circulate in the box.

To prevent escapes after the insect is in the box, seal the top and the bottom together with tape.

Don't keep any animal prisoner for too long. Allow the class to observe it, sketch it, and watch for changes, but once the study is done, put the insect back where you found it!

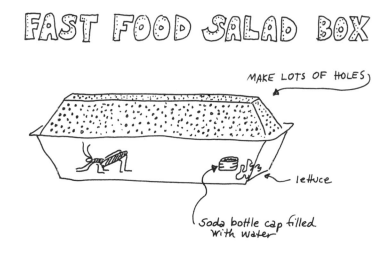

FAST FOOD SALAD BOX

MAKE LOTS OF HOLES

lettuce

Soda bottle cap filled with water

■■■■■■■■ WATER QUALITY SURVEY ■■■■■■■■

INTRODUCTION

So now you've made all sorts of equipment, what do you do with it? You can just have the kids find things in the water, observe them, sketch them and then do more research on what was found when they return to the classroom. But why not allow the class to act as real scientists? Conduct a stream survey to determine the environmental quality of the stream.

OVERVIEW

If the water happens to be a quick flowing stream or river, a "Benthic Organism Survey" is a means of determining the stream's environmental quality. Students work in teams to discover as many types of organisms as possible. The type and number of found animals are compared to the BIOTIC INDEX chart. The chart quickly enables the class to determine the environmental quality of the stream.

PROCEDURE

Materials

dip nets	pocket loupes/magnifiers
seining nets	insect field guides
collecting boxes	fish field guides
underwater viewing boxes	pencils and paper
clip boards	

1. Discuss necessary safety factors with the class.

   —Set the boundaries for the study.

   —Identify non-swimmers and make sure that they have land based or shallow water duties. (This should not be done in front of the rest of the class; there is no need to embarrass the children who simply haven't had the opportunity to learn to swim yet.)

   —Review safety rules for hip boot wearers.

2. Set up the research teams. Teams should include:

Dip net shallow water team	Rock search team
Seining net team	Water edge team

Biotic Index of Benthic Organisms

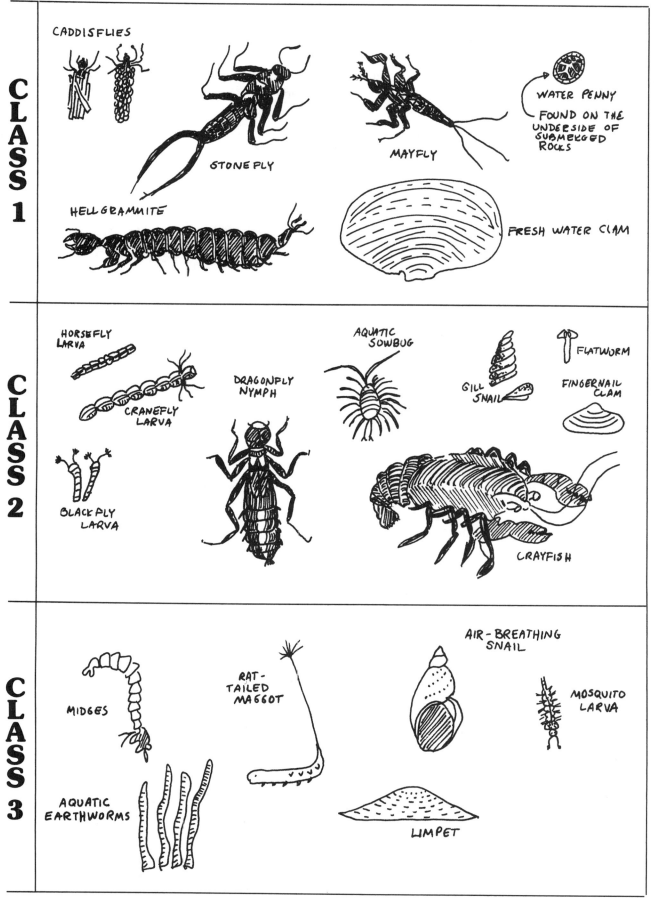

Depending on the number of students, you should have two or three students per team. Since most classes have more than 12 students, there will be two or three sets of research crews.

3. Discuss the procedure for using all of the equipment with the entire class.

4. Discuss the biotic index. Explain to the class that all of the organisms found in the index can be found in a clean stream. If only the Class 2 and Class 3 organisms are found, the stream has some pollution problems. If only the Class 3 organisms are found, the stream is polluted to a greater extent.

5. Decide on what the "everyone come here" signal should be. That way, when someone finds a treasure, it is easy to share the discovery with the whole class.

6. At the river or stream, try to have another responsible adult with a class if the number of students is over 20. There is a great deal of excitement and lots of wonderful discoveries at a river. If there is no other adult around, it will be hard to insure that the students stay on task.

7. When the survey is completed, discuss the organisms that were found. Have the class determine the quality of the stream using the biotic index.

8. Evaluate the activity with the class. Make sure that the students include what they liked, what they didn't like and give suggestions for improvement.

One time when we were conducting our river survey a boy who happened to be on the rock survey crew watched as an insect crawled up onto a rock. He thought that it was a water dwelling creature, so he decided to watch it for a minute to see what it was up to. It secured itself to the rock and it started to move so that its back started to split. He decided to call everyone, since it looked like this was going to be something unusual. As we watched, the insect pulled itself out of its body, leaving an empty shell attached to the rock. The insect's shape looked almost the same as the empty shell it had left behind. As time passed, the insect began to change shape. After an hour, it no longer looked at all like the shell it had left behind. We could see that it had wings, but we still weren't sure what it was. As the insect pumped blood into the wings, they extended farther and farther down the insect's body. Then, suddenly, the wings popped into place. We all exclaimed "…a dragonfly!" It was a wonderful experience for us to watch the nymph transform to an adult. When we returned to the classroom, the class was very eager to find out more about dragonflies. We all were enriched. The child who had first found the dragonfly acted like a proud father!

RESOURCES

Headstrom, Richard. *Adventures with Freshwater Animals*. New York: Dover Publications, Inc., 1964.

> This guide describes the behavior of insects and other living creatures that inhabit fresh water. It's a great guide for the

students. It is well-written and contains a great wealth of information.

The following are children's stories that deal with rivers:

Bellamy, David. *The River.* New York: Clarkson N. Potter, Inc./Publishers, 1988.

This beautifully illustrated book describes the plants, birds, fish, insects and amphibians that are found along a stream.

Cole, Joanna. *The Magic School Bus at the Waterworks.* New York: Scholastic Books Inc., 1986.

The water cycle is a part of the story of any stream or river. This delightful story should be a part of any river study.

Michl, Reinhard. *A Day on the River.* Barron's, Woodbury, New York, 1985.

This river trip is the tale of the adventures of three boys on a summer day. It is fun as well as descriptive of the flora and fauna found along a river.

PATTERNS FOUND IN NATURE

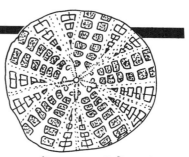

COMMON SAND DOLLAR

INTRODUCTION

Some patterns found in nature occur again and again. The pattern that a meandering stream traces in the earth is somewhat similar to the pattern the snake creates as it moves over the land. The branches of an oak tree look like the river system of a watershed, and sometimes like the branching of a bolt of lightning. Students search out these patterns to help enhance their observational skills.

OVERVIEW

Students must look for some common patterns found throughout their world. The class collects patterns and creates a display of common patterns and places they are found.

···PATTERN···	PLACES WHERE THE PATTERN IS FOUND:

PROCEDURE

1. Discuss some of the various patterns found in nature with the class.
2. Give each student one of the worksheets. Ask each student to find one subject that has the same pattern as each one on the worksheet.
3. Allow the students to complete the worksheet at home.
4. Draw each of the patterns on the board. Have the students discuss the objects that they found for each pattern.
5. Discuss the class findings and set up a committee of students to develop a display of the patterns that the class discovers.

EXTENSIONS

A great pattern book is called *Islamic Patterns,* by J. Bourgoin (Published by Dover Publications, Inc., New York, 1977). The book has 45 different patterns based on the geometrical patterns created by Muslim artists long ago.

Allow the students to look through the book and select one or two patterns. Duplicate the patterns selected and allow the students to color them in any way they wish. It is amazing how the same pattern can be colored in so many ways.

THINKING LIKE SCIENTISTS

TIME CAPSULE

INTRODUCTION

It's September, the first day of class. The classroom is filled with faces that mirror an incredible range of emotions. Some are wide-eyed, others are apprehensive, a few wear skeptical expressions and others just look down. It's important to set the tone for the year; you must be firm, but they need enthusiasm. Why not begin with an activity that they all will find interesting, involves scientific method, and will have them gathering information throughout the year? The culmination comes on the last day of the school year. Why not have each student create a personal time capsule?

OVERVIEW

Students fill out a form which requires that they predict what the year will be like. The students brainstorm some of the information, but standard questions are also a part of the form. The students record their weight and height, and each has his/her photo enclosed in the envelope containing their predictions for the year. At the end of the year, the class unseals the envelopes, and discovers how accurate their predictions were.

PROCEDURE

1. Duplicate the TIME CAPSULE form and discuss it with the students.
2. Ask the class if they can think of any other information which should be included. Write suggestions on the board, and discuss whether or not the suggestions should be included in the time capsule.
3. Have the class complete the forms. Photograph each student. Ask each to seal the form and photo in an envelope with that student's name written on the outside. Place all of the envelopes in a large manilla envelope or some other large container that will hold all of the envelopes.
4. Place the container in a closet, or someplace where it will be safe until the end of the school year.
5. Create a large poster with the topics of the time capsule written on it. As the answer for each topic becomes evident, fill in the chart. That way, in June, the answers can be verified.
6. When the students open the time capsules, they may wish to fill out another form, this one for the *NEXT* year! Repeat the whole process and then at the end of the next year make sure that the students get their time capsules!

TIME CAPSULE QUESTIONNAIRE

Name_____

Date_____

Nickname_____Height_____

Weight_____

Best friends_____

_____

_____

_____

Favorite pastimes_____

_____

_____

Favorite books	Favorite songs	Favorite music groups
Favorite sport	**Favorite pro sports team**	**Favorite college sports team**

Favorite meal_____

Favorite color_____

PREDICTIONS

1. On Christmas, the weather will be _____

2. The high temperature for New Year's Day will be _____

3. The first day in the new year that the temperature will reach 60°F will be _____

_____

4. The temperature at the time I open this will be _____

5. My predictions about technology: _____

_____

_____

_____

6. My predictions about the environment and related laws or activities:

_____

_____

_____

GOALS

1. My goals for this year are_____

_____

_____

_____

2. In order to attain those goals, I need to_____

_____

_____

_____

_____

3. Eventually, I'd like to become a _____

4. I look forward to participating in the following this year:

_____

_____

_____

_____

5. If I could change one thing, I'd change_____

_____

_____

_____

EXTENSIONS

A friend of mine uses this delayed technique to remind students in a graduate course of their goals and aspirations...years after they have taken her course. Each semester, she asks the students to write down their immediate goals and their long term goals. They seal the list in an envelope with their address written on the outside and give the envelope to the professor. After four or five years have passed, she mails them out! It is a message from the person they used to be!

A Real Time Capsule

Have the class create a real time capsule for the students who will sit in their seats 100 years from now.

1. Have the class discuss what they think future generations will think of them.

2. Ask what things that we have now will be symbolic of us 100 years from now.

3. What would each student say to a student in their grade 100 years from now?

4. What are the things that the students consider to be the "latest advances?" (Motorized computer chips, superconductors, etc.) If the class has trouble identifying current advances, copies of "Popular Science" magazine, and other science-oriented magazines should contain many ideas for the students.
   After listing as many advances as possible, ask the class which ones should be included in the time capsule.

5. Have the class predict what they think the houses and cities that will exist 100 years from now will be like. Ask the students to draw pictures and label them.

6. Ask the class to determine what other things should be included? Copies of tapes and music? Fashion magazines? A television schedule? A copy of a textbook? What else?

7. When all of the materials have been collected, what next? Perhaps the local library would be willing to house the capsule. Maybe it can be placed in a waterproof container, sealed and then buried somewhere where people 100 years from now can find it. Have the class suggest other possibilities and decide on the best one.

A Backwards Time Capsule

Ask the class to create a time capsule for themselves, pretending that they are students who attended school 100 years ago. They should include all of the things that they would include in the real time capsule. Research is of the essence for this project!

History buffs and experts in technology of the past are good prospective guest speakers, if this task is undertaken! The *Little House On the Prairie* books by Laura Ingalls Wilder might be helpful for the class to get a feeling of the era! You may wish to read one or two of the books aloud to the class.

READING ALOUD

Reading aloud to the class is important. Many students don't have much opportunity to listen to good stories and picture the events of the story in their minds. Television and movies don't allow the students to create their own visuals. Reading aloud does. A few years ago, we decided to try a read aloud program at our grades 6-8 middle school. A number of teachers gave up one planning period per week and went to the library to read the story of their choice aloud to any study hall students who wanted to listen.

After we announced the program, we posted a list of who was reading which book and when they were reading it. Naturally the books that I selected always had a science focus. *A Wrinkle in Time* by Madeline L'Engle (Dell Publishing Co., 1962), *Island of the Blue Dolphins* by Scott O'Dell (Houghton Mifflin, 1965), *Julie of the Wolves* by Jean Craighead George (Harper and Row, 1972), and *The Bread Sister* by Robin Moore (Groundhog Press, 1984) are a few of the books that I selected.

We tape recorded each story for absentees and to develop a "books on tape" file. The program was a huge success! Students for all three grade levels attended and loved the chance to listen to a good story. Students who wanted to hear a story but didn't have a study hall at the time it was being read could always listen to the tape.

I didn't realize how important the program was to the students until the day I forgot to go to the library. They came to get me! And they were annoyed that I had wasted some of their listening time! I never forgot again.

▬▬ SEATING CHART SLEUTHING ▬▬

INTRODUCTION

One activity to incorporate thinking skills into a science lesson is based on your seating chart. We *all* know teachers who seat their students by alphabetical order, and this activity is based on that concept, but the students need to determine how you went about creating the seating order.

OVERVIEW

Based on information obtained from a questionnaire, students are assigned certain seats in the classroom. Students develop theories as to why they are seated as they are. Through discussion and testing those theories, the students determine the seating arrangement order.

Name_____ Date_____

QUESTIONNAIRE

Please fill out this questionnaire. Some of the questions are easy and some are hard and require much thought. The best way to fill this out is to read through the whole set, answering the easy questions as you go. Then go back to the beginning and answer the harder questions. Take your time; don't rush. Please have these in my mailbox on my desk by:_____.

1. What is your full name?_____

2. How many brothers and sisters do you have? Please name them and give their ages._____

_____

_____

3. What is your favorite food?_____

_____

4. What smell do you dislike the most?_____

5. What is your favorite color?_____

6. Which sport do you enjoy the most?_____

7. How do you spend your free time?_____

_____

8. When is your birthday?_____

9. Which animal are you most like? Why do you think so?_____

_____

10. Who do you think is going to win the World Series?_____

11. What is the title of the best book that you've ever read?

_____

12. Which subject do you enjoy the most at school? (Lunch doesn't count!)_____

13. Since you can be anything that you want to when you grow up, (as long as you work hard) what do you want to be when you are 25 years old?_____

14. What is the best thing about the outdoors?_____

_____

15. Which animal would you most like to see?_____

16. What do you do that you consider to be the most important thing you do?_____

_____

17. What do you hope to study in science this year?_____

_____

_____

18. What is your favorite dream?_____

_____

_____

PROCEDURE

1. As a beginning of the year activity, students complete a questionnaire which will give you the information you need to arrange the students in unusual groupings.

2. A week or two later, arrange the class according to the seating chart developed as a result of the questionnaire.

For Example:

   —Arrange the class in alphabetical order using their oldest sibling's first name.

   —Use their birth month, seating the December birthdays first, the November birthdays next and so on.

3. Challenge the class to create theories as to the underlying information that determines the seating order.

4. Change the seating arrangement three or four more times during the year, each time using different criteria for seating.

■■■■■■■■■■ BUT WILL IT WORK? ■■■■■■■■■■

INTRODUCTION

As educators, we are always on the lookout for new ideas, experiments and projects to try to make our classes more exciting. One thing may sound wonderful, but when we actually have the kids try it, it doesn't seem to work as it should. "But Will It Work?" is an activity that takes a look at some of these projects and experiments. The activity also requires the students to think, predict and verify their results.

OVERVIEW

Each student selects one experiment or project and explains it to the class. After each project is explained, students predict whether they feel that the experiment or project will be successful or not when it is actually demonstrated to the class.

After the class makes their predictions, students set up the criteria for success or failure of a particular project. The project is then tested, and evaluated as to its success or failure.

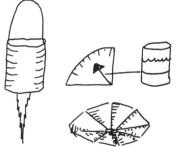

Name_____ Date_____

? ? ? ? ? ? ? ? ? **BUT WILL IT WORK?**   ? ? ? ? ? ? ? ?
MY PREDICTIONS

DATE	EXPERIMENT	STUDENT	WILL IT WORK?

? ? ? ? ? ? ? ? ? **BUT WILL IT WORK?**   ? ? ? ? ? ? ? ?
MY PREDICTIONS

PROCEDURE

1. Create a list of projects with instructions for the class as a beginning point for the class. If time allows, let the students look through old science text books written for their level to find experiments. Students may select a project from your list, from an old text, or they can locate one on their own. Before beginning any project or experiment, students need to check with the teacher to make sure that it is an appropriate one.

2. Allow students a few days to decide which project they wish to undertake. As they are deciding, make sure that the project or experiment is safe, within the student's ability to carry out, and has a reasonable chance for success.

3. On the day each student needs to announce which project he/she has selected for presentation, make sure that each student is prepared to answer the following questions:

   —What is the experiment/project?

   —What is the purpose of the experiment?

   —How will he/she carry out the project/experiment?

   —What materials will be needed?

   —What assistance will be needed?

   —How much time will be needed for the project/experiment to be prepared?

NOTE: As each project is explained, listen for safety factors and precautions. After each presentation, ask the class whether or not there are any safety concerns with the proposed project or experiment. Ask the student to modify any dangerous experiments. If necessary, ask that student to select a different project.

4. Duplicate the chart BUT WILL IT WORK?. You should have one chart per student. As each student presents his/her project or experiment, students record their predictions for whether or not they think each will work.

5. After all of the presentations have been made and all of the predictions have been recorded, collect the charts and store them in a safe place until all of the experiments and projects have been conducted.

6. Create a large chart that lists the project, the date it is to be presented, and a blank column for noting whether it is successful.

7. Projects and experiments need to be tested in a scientific manner. Make sure that everyone knows what the project is supposed to do. Before testing, establish what will constitute successful performance and what will constitute failure. Try the project more than once if necessary.

8. When all of the projects have been completed, return the prediction sheets to the students. Using the large chart, they can determine how accurate their predictions were.

9. When evaluating the project, have the class determine their overall success rate.

10. A fitting end for the whole process is to give out awards to the students. Make sure that each student receives a certificate! Categories might include:

—Best Unsuccessful Experiment

—Most Creative Design

—Best Explanation

—Neatest Project

—Most Decorative Project

—Best Designed Project That Worked

—Best Designed Project That Didn't Work

—Most Organized Experiment

—Most Creative/Safest Storage Container

NOTE: As the experiments and projects are being presented, keep in mind that certificates will be handed out at the end of this activity. Watch for unusual happenings to reward students for hard work, creative thinking, kindness to others, and other positive happenings. Some suggestions for experiments:

—Make a homemade barometer by stretching a balloon over the neck of a jar. A straw is then attached to the balloon. The straw points to a graph to determine the air pressure.

—Solar cookers made from cardboard and aluminum foil.

—Baking soda/vinegar volcanoes.

—Hummingbird feeder that is made from a jar with a hole punched in the top.

—Solar hand warmers. These look like mini solar cookers.

—In winter, make an icicle by punching a hole in the bottom of a can, putting water in the can so that the resultant dripping water forms an icicle.

—Collecting oxygen from underwater plants by inverting a water-filled test tube over the plants.

A TOWERING SUCCESS

INTRODUCTION

Math skills merge with engineering skills as students attempt to build the tallest structure using materials purchased from the central supply warehouse. Accurate accounting is a must for structures with cost overruns are disqualified.

OVERVIEW

Students design and construct structures that can support two hardback dictionaries. The tallest structure is the one determined to be the winner.

1. Introduce the activity to the class by handing each student a "Wanted... Structure Construction Crew" flyer. Read through the rules:

   —The crew must create a structure that is as tall as possible, but must be able to support two dictionaries. (Have the dictionaries on hand for the group to see. Make sure that they are available for testing purposes throughout the construction time.)

   —Structure construction materials must be purchased by "Central Supply" purchase order only.

   —A structure cannot cost more than $2,400,000.

   —All construction crew financial records will be audited prior to the testing of the strength of the structure.

   —Cost overruns will disqualify the structure.

   —The tallest structure that meets all conditions will be declared the winner!

   —All structures must be completed on time and according to the specifications.

2. Discuss the project and divide the class so that each construction crew has four or five students.

3. Hand each group one price list, and review the costs of the materials that will be used. Point out that only materials from Central Supply can be used.

   Full Straw . . . . $ 40,000

   Half Straw. . . . . $ 25,000

   Paperclip . . . . $ 20,000

   12″ masking tape . . . . $ 5,000

   Glue/day. . . . . $ 8,000

Name_____ Date_____

Each crew will:

• create the tallest possible structure that will support *two* standard-sized dictionaries.

• have a budget of $2,400,000.

• keep complete, accurate records.

• purchase their supplies from "Central Supply Company" *ONLY*.

• complete the structure on time *and* within budget.

• the tallest structure will be declared the winning structure!

CENTRAL SUPPLY COMPANY

★ PRICE LIST: ★

Full Straw.............. $40,000
Half Straw.............. $25,000
Paperclip $20,000
12" Masking Tape..... $ 5,000
Glue/day............. $ 8,000
Toothpick............. $10,000
Half Toothpick........ $ 6,000
Shipping Container.. $ 2,000

All prices are subject to change.

Toothpick . . . .$ 10,000

Half toothpick. . . . .$ 6,000

Shipping container . . . .$ 2,000

NOTE:

—Use paper straws, not plastic ones. The plastic ones bend too readily.

—The shipping container is a paper bag the size of a lunchbag.

4. The crews should create names for their groups. Next, have the groups decide on which member(s) will be the accountant(s). It is very important that accurate records be kept. If the crew doesn't stay within budget, they will be disqualified.

5. Allow the students to begin designing structures. After they have been working for a while, ask them where they can get more ideas. Hopefully they will try the library, direct observation of structures that already exist, and information from people who are in the business of building real structures: engineers, architects, etc.

6. Create a bulletin board that has a file folder stapled to it for incoming orders. It also should have a price list and rules for the project.

7. Make sure that all orders received before class begins are filled before the students come to class.

8. Management tips for the teacher:

—Label one file folder for each construction crew.

—Whenever you receive an order, place the form in the folder.

—When you fill each order, check the prices for accuracy and add up the total. Keep a running total on the front of the file folder for your own information. It is a means for you to check the students' accuracy as the project proceeds.

—If you find a discrepancy, point it out to the crew's accountant.

9. Allow two weeks for this project. On the day before the projects are due, ask each group's accountant to submit their records. Check their records with the file folder records. If there is a discrepancy, ask the accountant to rework the figures so that they are accurate. Do not allow any group to test their structure until the records are correct.

10. Invite parents and other interested adults to attend the structure testing. It's a fun time for all!

11. On testing day, have each group present their structure, and explain how it was designed and why the group selected that design.

12. Test each structure, placing the dictionaries in the place provided. Make sure that safety factors have been considered. If necessary, borrow a janitor's ladder, rather than having students standing on top of desks.

CENTRAL SUPPLY OFFICIAL ORDER FORM

Construction Crew Name: _____

Date: _____

Order Number: _____

Name of Item	How Many?	Price for One	Total Price

SHIPPING METHOD:

		Total Price
Total Cost for Supplies		
New shipping container ($2,000)	+	
Recycled shipping container ($0)		
Express service ($500)	+	
CREDIT FOR RETURNED MATERIALS	−	
TOTAL FOR SUPPLIES AND SHIPPING		

For Office Use Only

Date Order Received _____

Order Filled By _____

Order Shipped On _____

(Prices subject to change without notice.)

NOTE: Some groups will quickly find alternatives to placing the dictionaries on top of their structures! The rules state that the structure simply needs to support two dictionaries. Encourage the groups to work in secrecy so that original ideas are allowed to flourish!

13. When the structures have all been tested, and the winners are determined, give each winning group member a certificate. Reward other groups that displayed creative thinking or diligent work with certificates as well.

14. Make sure that the students evaluate the project. Discuss what they liked, what they didn't like, and what suggestions that they have for improvements. If the

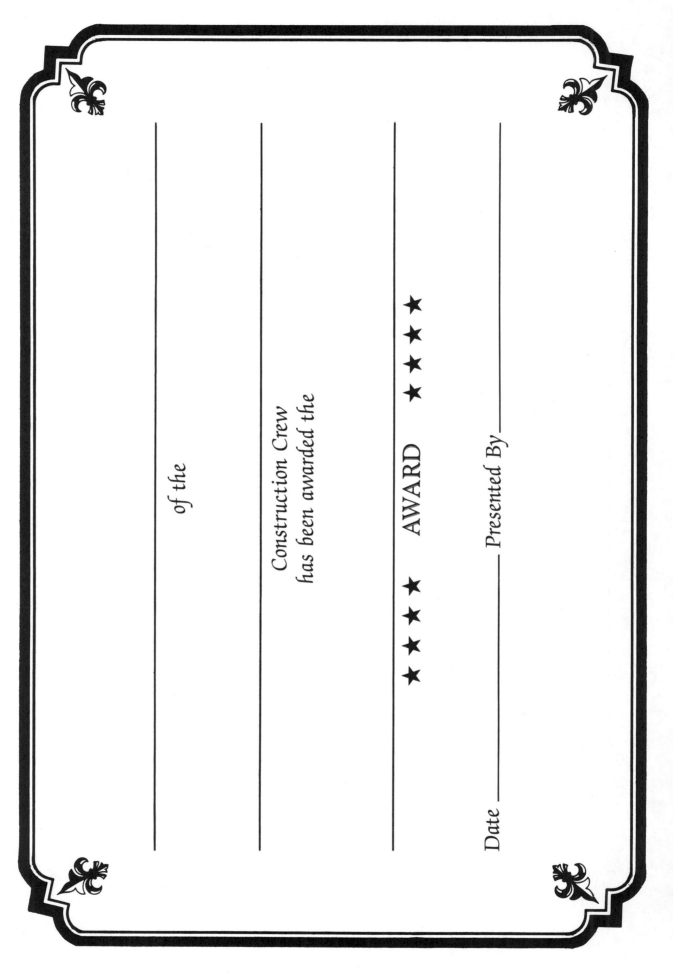

of the

Construction Crew
has been awarded the

★ ★ ★   AWARD   ★ ★ ★

Presented By

Date

suggestions are appropriate, *write down the changes* so that the next time you attempt this project, you know how it should be modified to make it better!

EXTENSIONS

1. Another building material can be made from newspapers. Take a toothpick and place it on a corner of an opened piece of newspaper. Roll the paper tightly around the toothpick, and tape the completed roll. The rolled paper will be very strong and the students can build big structures with it.

   The complete newspaper/toothpick lesson is described in *Scienceworks,* which is put out with the Ontario Science Centre and published by Addison-Wesley Publishing Company, Inc., Reading, MA, 1984, used here by permission. It is a great activity book!

2. Challenge the class to develop other recycled building materials. The class might brainstorm materials and then predict which materials will be the sturdiest. The class should then develop a means for testing the various materials.

THE SEVEN TASK PROJECT

INTRODUCTION

Students need to learn how the scientific process works. When presented with a problem, most of the time, scientists use a definite course of action normally called the scientific method. Solving a problem which is unknown, a mystery, leads to much more than an exercise in real science. It leads to the development of strategies to solve other problems, a boost in self esteem, an analysis of thought processes, and the excitement of meeting a challenge and succeeding.

The SEVEN TASK PROJECT is a program which enables the students to truly think as scientists think. There is no authority to go to for the answer because the solution has yet to be found. Students may go to resources to research some ideas, they may turn to teachers, parents and other adults to help brainstorm possible solutions, but until they actually create the solution, they have no idea whether or not their idea will work. They keep a notebook of trials and modifications made, just as a scientist would. They present their results to their peers and the results must be able to be duplicated.

OVERVIEW

Students are presented with seven physical problems. They have two months to prepare a solution which meets the requirements of one of the seven problems. They spend one class period per week working on solving their problem. When the solutions are presented to the class, parents are invited in to observe the solutions.

The program is one which allows all students to develop their ability to solve problems. It forces students to stretch themselves and think. It creates excitement in the classroom as students use critical thinking skills, problem solving technique and higher order thinking skills.

PROCEDURE

1. After a discussion of the ways in which scientists solve problems, announce that the students are about to act like real scientists and that they are going to solve problems which are pretty tough because no one has ever faced these problems before.

2. Read through the seven problems listed for this project with the students. Different problems than the ones listed here most certainly may be created, but they should be of a similar nature. They should be open-ended, but well defined, including the parameters and guidelines. Students need to work out the basics for themselves, just as a scientist must.

3. Students should each receive a copy of the seven problems so that they can decide which one they wish to work on.

The problems are:

> —Construct a water transfer device. It must transfer 2 liters of water from one container to another one, at least 5m away, with a loss of water no greater than .05 liters. No siphons or hands are allowed. Movement must be made by mechanical means, although hand-powered devices may be created.

> —Devise a means of crossing a 10m stretch of snow/mud without leaving tracks.

> —Create a wake-up device that makes no sound.

> —Build a camera obscura and photograph something that is invisible.

> —Construct a device that does three different things or movements at the same time.

> —Construct a device that moves a ball from one spot to another spot 2 meters directly above it. "Spots" may be constructed, but they cannot move. Hands may only be used to set the device for movement into motion.

> —Create a combination sundial/windsock that is all one piece.

4. But there are problems within the problems! It is necessary for the student to keep in mind that only recycled materials can be used.

5. Another aspect of the project is that students need to consider the logistics of getting their projects to school. If the majority of students ride school busses, it is imperative that the project not weigh tons or be so unwieldy that it doesn't fit

through the bus doors. Some students who find that their project won't fit on the bus might have willing parents who will drive the projects to school, but the project still must fit in the car!

6. Students can have parental guidance, but this is the student's project. The notebook that the students keep with ideas, successes, failures, and thoughts for improving the project is the important part of the project. Since it is checked and worked on in class each week, checking insures that students are doing the work themselves. It is through this weekly conferring and checking that the real progress in thought is made. Students must have new material added to their notebooks each week. Each notebook is initialed at the end of the weekly conference. Not only does this help in maintaining that the students are thinking and working, there is no way a student can create a project the night before it is due. Students are assured frequently that the success of the project is not as important as the notebook. Projects that don't work can still get a good grade. The notebook is the means of recording the process of solving the problem which is what counts. It is unfortunate that grades must be assigned to this project at all, but the reality of school situations is that if there is no grade attached to the project, a few students will not take the project seriously.

7. Some of the tasks are much easier than others, and students are allowed to switch tasks within the first two weeks of the project. After that, they must stick to the problem they have selected.

8. About one week before the projects are to be presented to the class, a list of the order in which problems will be presented is posted. This enables students to plan accordingly, and all project solutions for a specific problem are due on the same day. This rule prevents students from copying good ideas from someone else's project. When all projects of the same type have been presented, they must be taken home to make room for the next batch of projects.

9. Each project is evaluated by a prepared checklist for each specific problem. (See the end of this unit.) Each student is given an evaluation form as soon as they select the problem on which they will work.

10. The actual project work is done at home. This insures that original designs and ideas are not copied by other students, intentionally or not. Students are also encouraged not to share ideas with others working on the same project. Working at home also enables parents to be a part of the project, but the notebooks insure that they aren't doing the project for the student.

11. On each form there are two sections: the notebook and the project. The notebook evaluation is the same for all projects. This section is worth 60 percent of the total grade. The project section is based on the rules which govern each project and determine success by the number of rules and guidelines that have been followed. This section is 40 percent of the total grade.

THE SEVEN TASK PROJECT

You may choose one of the following projects, or you may create your own task. If you create your own, you must have it okayed prior to beginning work on it! You will keep a detailed notebook so that you don't lose any of your thoughts, ideas, or sketches! The notebook will be as important as the project! Here are the seven tasks:

Choose One

1. Construct a water transfer device. It must transfer 2 liters of water from one container to another one, at least 5 meters away, with a loss of water no greater than .05L. No siphons or hands are allowed. Movement must be made by mechanical means, although hand-powered devices may be created.

2. Devise a means of crossing a 10m stretch of snow/mud without leaving tracks.

3. Create a wake-up device that makes no sound.

4. Build a camera obscura and photograph something that is invisible.

5. Construct a device that does three different things or movements at the same time.

6. Construct a device that moves a ball from one spot to another spot 2m directly above it. "Spots" may be constructed, but they cannot move. Hands may only be used to set the device for movement into motion.

7. Create a combination sundial/windsock that is all one piece.

© 1990 by The Center for Applied Research in Education

Name_____ Date_____

Water Transfer

NOTEBOOKS:

1. Are at least three ideas stated? . . . . ._____

2. Are predictions for each idea listed? . . . . ._____

3. Are models/sketches drawn for each idea? . . . . ._____

4. Are the results of each trial stated? . . . . ._____

5. Are ways to make the project work better listed? . . . . ._____

6. Is the final paragraph which details how the final project meets all the specifications of the project included? . . . . ._____

Each of the notebook items has a 0 - 10 point value. Total notebook value is 60% of the total grade.

PROJECTS:

Water Transfer:

7. Does the device work? . . . . ._____

8. Does it lose less than .05L of water? . . . . ._____

9. Are the containers 5m apart? . . . . ._____

10. Is the movement of water within all rules? . . . . ._____

11. Is the project neatly prepared? . . . . ._____

Each of the project items has a 0 - 5 point value with the exception of #10, which has a 0 - 20 point value. Total project value is 40% of the total grade.

Crossing the Snow

NOTEBOOKS:

1. Are at least three ideas stated? . . . . ._____

2. Are predictions for each idea listed? . . . . ._____

3. Are models/sketches drawn for each idea? . . . . ._____

4. Are the results of each trial stated? . . . . ._____

5. Are ways to make the project work better listed? . . . . ._____

6. Is the final paragraph which details how the final project meets all the specifications of the project included? . . . . ._____

Each of the notebook items has a 0 - 10 point value. Total notebook value is 60% of the total grade.

PROJECTS:

Crossing the Snow:

7. Does the device work? . . . . ._____

8. Is all evidence of prints gone? . . . . ._____

9. Are there any disturbances in the snow as a result of the snow crossing project? . . . . . ._____

10. Is the movement across the snow within all rules? . . . . ._____

11. Is the project neatly prepared? . . . . ._____

Each of the project items has a 0 - 5 point value with the exception of #10, which has a 0 - 20 point value. Total project value is 40% of the total grade.

Name_____ Date_____

Wake Up!

NOTEBOOKS:

1. Are at least three ideas stated? . . . . ._____

2. Are predictions for each idea listed? . . . . ._____

3. Are models/sketches drawn for each idea? . . . . ._____

4. Are the results of each trial stated? . . . . ._____

5. Are ways to make the project work better listed? . . . . ._____

6. Is a final paragraph which details how the final project meets all the specifications
   of the project included? . . . . ._____

Each of the notebook items has a 0 - 10 point value. Total notebook value is 60% of the total grade.

PROJECTS:

Wake Up:

7. Does it make any sound? . . . . ._____

8. Can it awaken a person at a set time? . . . . ._____

9. Does it harm the person in any way? . . . . ._____

10. Does the project conform to all rules? . . . . ._____

11. Is the project neatly prepared? . . . . ._____

Each of the project items has a 0 - 5 pont value with the exception of #10, which has a 0 - 20 point value. Total project value is 40% of the total grade.

Photograph the Invisible

NOTEBOOKS:

1. Are at least three ideas stated? . . . . ._____

2. Are predictions for each idea listed? . . . . ._____

3. Are models/sketches drawn for each idea? . . . . ._____

4. Are the results of each trial stated? . . . . ._____

5. Are ways to make the project work better listed? . . . . ._____

6. Is a final paragraph which details how the final project meets all the specifications of the project included? . . . . ._____

Each of the notebook items has a 0 - 10 point value. Total notebook value is 60% of the total grade.

PROJECTS:

Photograph the Invisible:

7. Does the camera work? . . . . ._____

8. Can the student accurately describe how the camera works? . . . . ._____

9. Is the object photographed invisible? . . . . ._____

10. Does the project conform to all rules? . . . . ._____

11. Is the camera neatly prepared? . . . . ._____

Each of the project items has a 0 - 5 point value with the exception of #10, which has a 0 - 20 point value. Total project value is 40% of the total grade.

© 1990 by The Center for Applied Research in Education

Name_____ Date_____

Triple Motion

NOTEBOOKS:

1. Are at least three ideas stated? . . . . ._____

2. Are predictions for each idea listed? . . . . ._____

3. Are models/sketches drawn for each idea? . . . . ._____

4. Are the results of each trial stated? . . . . ._____

5. Are ways to make the project work better listed? . . . . ._____

6. Is a final paragraph which details how the final project meets all the specifications
   of the project included? . . . . ._____

Each of the notebook items has a 0 - 10 point value. Total notebook value is 60% of the total grade.

PROJECTS:

Triple Motion:

7. Is each movement different? . . . . ._____

8. Do all movements occur at the same time? . . . . ._____

9. Are the motions started by one device? . . . . ._____

10. Does the project conform to all rules? . . . . ._____

11. Is it neatly prepared? . . . . ._____

Each of the project items has a 0 - 5 point value with the exception of #10, which has a 0 - 20 point value. Total project value is 40% of the total grade.

Name_____ Date_____

Moving Spheres

NOTEBOOKS:

1. Are at least three ideas stated? . . . . ——

2. Are predictions for each idea listed? . . . . ——

3. Are models/sketches drawn for each idea? . . . . ——

4. Are the results of each trial stated? . . . . ——

5. Are ways to make the project work better listed? . . . . ——

6. Is a final paragraph which details how the final project meets all the
   specifications of the project included? . . . . ——

Each of the notebook items has a 0 - 10 point value. Total notebook value is
60% of the total grade.

PROJECTS:

Moving Spheres:

7. Does the ball remain in place at the top? . . . . ——

8. Is the ball exactly 2m above its starting point? . . . . ——

9. Are hand movements used only to start the device? . . . . ——

10. Does the project conform to all rules? . . . . ——

11. Is the project neatly prepared? . . . . ——

Each of the project items has a 0 - 5 point value with the exception of #10,
which has a 0 - 20 point value. Total project value is 40% of the total grade.

Windsock/Sundial

NOTEBOOKS:

1. Are at least three ideas stated? . . . . ._____

2. Are predictions for each idea listed? . . . . ._____

3. Are models/sketches drawn for each idea? . . . . ._____

4. Are the results of each trial stated? . . . . ._____

5. Are ways to make the project work better listed? . . . . ._____

6. Is a final paragraph which details how the final project meets all the specifications
   of the project included? . . . . ._____

Each of the notebook items has a 0 - 10 point value. Total notebook value is 60% of the total grade.

PROJECTS:

Windsock/Sundial:

7. Does the sundial accurately tell time? . . . . ._____

8. Does the windsock indicate wind direction? . . . . ._____

9. Can the student explain how the sundial works? . . . . ._____

10. Does the project conform to all rules? . . . . ._____

11. Is the project neatly prepared? . . . . ._____

Each of the project items has a 0 - 5 point value with the exception of #10, which has a 0 - 20 point value. Total project value is 40% of the total grade.

WORDS, WORDS, WORDS

INTRODUCTION

Written language is a means by which we communicate with others, as well as a means of understanding the thoughts and ideas of people of the past. It is a means by which we can communicate with people of the future. Yet, just how accurate are the words that we use? As scientists, it is imperative that we learn to express ourselves accurately. This is an experience in which students learn the importance of careful observation and accurate words.

OVERVIEW

This activity really allows parents to participate in the fun and learning of the students. Students are asked to create a written description of a modern art sculpture which is made from ordinary classroom objects. The assignment for the evening is to have the parents draw the sculpture from the student's description. The results make the meaning of accuracy in description very real to both students and their parents!

PROCEDURE

1. Using lab equipment, odds and ends and other stuff hanging around, construct a complex sculpture of various pieces of equipment that resembles a modern art sculpture.

2. Have the "sculpture" covered as students come into the room. Announce that scientists need many tools to work, but one of the most important tools is the skill to use words accurately. Discuss why this skill is important with the class.

3. After the discussion, play a few rounds of a game where one student is blindfolded, another student describes an object in the classroom, and the blindfolded student has two chances to guess what the object is. After each round, discuss which clues were most effective.

4. Have the class focus on the covered sculpture. Announce that it is time to put their descriptive skills to the test, and have the students describe the sculpture in writing. Remind them to do their very best. The students should not name any object. For example, students might call a tongue depressor "a flattened wooden slab with rounded ends, approximately five inches long."

5. When everyone has completed their descriptions, hand each student a piece of drawing paper. Ask the students to read their descriptions to either their parents, an older brother or sister, or a neighbor. The parent should draw the object that they picture in their minds as a result of the description. No extra words can be added, and students may not coach the parents as to the correct way to draw something. They may only read the description that they have written. They may read it more than once, but they cannot add anything else. Each artist should sign his/her artwork.

6. The next time that you meet, share the drawings with the class. Each student should read his/her description and then show the class the drawing that was made as a result of the written description.

7. Discuss which words were the most accurate. You might even award prizes for the various masterpieces. Aside from the obvious "Most Realistic," "Most Creative," you might wish to add fun categories such as "Most likely to give a person nightmares," "Most likely to be found in Dracula's living room," or whatever.

8. This is a great activity for a time when the parents are coming to school such as an "Open House," or "Back to School Night." Post the drawings with the descriptions. Keep the sculpture intact so the parents can see what it really looks like. It gives the parents something to look for as well as the opportunity to see the results of other's efforts.

KALEIDOSCOPES LARGE...

INTRODUCTION

When studying light, why not create a giant Kaleidoscope from inexpensive mirrors? The cost is low and the excitement that such a delightful piece of equipment generates is high.

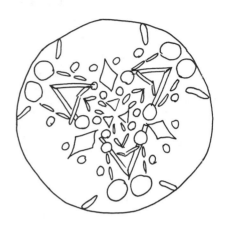

OVERVIEW

The class creates a giant Kaleidoscope from three large mirrors. By changing the configuration of the mirrors, the class should be able to generate different patterns. The class should generate predictions as to how the pattern will change.

PROCEDURE

1. Purchase three inexpensive full length mirrors from a discount store. Buy the kind that have no frame.
2. Using duct tape, tape the three mirrors together along the sides.
3. Using heavy cardboard, wood or some other substance, cut out a large circle that covers the end of the mirror triangle. Cut a smaller hole in the center of the large circle for viewing.
4. When you are ready to use the Kaleidoscope, place it on a large table facing a window or other source of light.
5. Place an object or even a student's face at the other end of the Kaleidoscope and have another student look through the small hole of the circle.
*NOTE: Make sure that safety is stressed with this lesson. If students are changing the angle of the mirrors, make sure that two students are manipulating the mirrors from each end while another student looks through the viewer.
6. When the class has had a chance to experiment with the giant Kaleidoscope for a time, ask them to predict what the pattern will be like if the triangular configuration of the mirrors is made smaller.
7. Make the end triangle shape of the mirrors smaller, and have the class verify their predictions, and then have the class predict what should happen if the triangular shape is made greater.
8. Make the triangles of the Kaleidoscope larger and, once again, have the class verify the results.

9. Discuss the students' observations and ask the class to generate explanations for the findings.
10. If the class has any other suggestions for experiments with the giant Kaleidoscope, have the students design how the experiment should be set up, and then carry out the plan.

EXTENSIONS

—Discuss the angle of reflection and the results of changes in the configuration. Then have the class experiment with the way light changes when it passes through water. Use an aquarium or large glass jar and have the class note the way submerged objects seem to be "slightly off" from where they should be!

—Have the students shine flashlights into the water to see what the water does with a beam of light. Put different colored cellophane over the lens of the flashlights to determine whether different colors have any effect on the way the light is reflected and refracted.

—Place a mirror at a 30 degree angle in a bowl of water. Shine a flashlight at the mirror. A rainbow will appear on the ceiling! This experiment was first done by Sir Isaac Newton. If the spectrum on the ceiling isn't bright enough, darken the room.

—Find prisms with which the class can experiment. Let the class members set up their own experiments.

...AND KALEIDOSCOPES SMALL.

INTRODUCTION

This time the kaleidoscope is used in an entirely different way. It is used to have the students simulate how an insect with compound eyes sees the world. Although this isn't exactly the way in which compound eyes work, the class can determine how the effects of looking through the small kaleidoscope are similar and different from the way a compound-eyed insect sees!

OVERVIEW

Using duct tape, students tape three small mirrors together to make small kaleidoscopes. Then, the class investigates how animals with compound eyes see. They also investigate how real the kaleidoscope comes to simulating the way that insects with compound eyes see.

PROCEDURE

1. Provide three small mirrors for each kaleidoscope needed. The mirrors should be rectangular with the length at least four times greater than the width. Duct tape will be needed to tape the mirrors together.
2. Divide the class into small working groups.
3. Demonstrate how to tape the mirrors together. (Tape the mirrored parts toward the inside of the triangle.)
4. Allow the class time to look through the small kaleidoscopes and experiment with them.
5. Ask the class to imagine that they are insects with compound eyes. Ask the students in which ways the kaleidoscopes seem like compound eyes and in what ways the kaleidoscopes seem different.
6. List the responses on the board as they are suggested. Ask one of the students to write the responses on paper, so after the research has been completed, the class can determine how close they were to reality.
7. Have the class research the ways in which insects see and compare the findings to their original thoughts.
A good book on the subject is *How Animals See* by Sandra Sinclair (Croom Helm Ltd., Kent, England, 1985).

EXTENSIONS

—Divide the class into groups to research the way that different insects and animals see. Some suggestions for study might be:

—hawk	—squirrel
—cat	—dog
—owl	—polar bear
—frog	—mountain goat
—whale	—jellyfish
—honeybee	—bat
—preying mantis	—garter snake
—orb web weaving spider	—robin
—jumping spider	—trout
—luna moth	—black bear

—Have the class do research to discover the vision of the dinosaurs. What animals today might give the class clues as to the sight of the dinosaurs?

DISCOVER SUNDIALS!

OVERVIEW

Have the class make sundials outside on the playground or in the parking lot. All you need is chalk and two students. One will be the sundial and the other will trace the sundial's shadow every hour on the hour. At the end of the day, we have a complete sundial for the school day.

PROCEDURE

1. Discuss time-keeping devices of the past and the problems that were associated with them.
2. Announce that the class is about to embark on a sundial project.
3. Select the two students who will be the "sundial" and the "shadow sketcher." (If you wish, you can have the class form groups of two and each group can make a sundial.)
4. Have the students mark the playground or some other hard surface with an "X" with the chalk.
5. The student who is the "sundial" stands on that "X" each time his/her shadow is to be sketched.
6. Every hour have the two students go outdoors and sketch the perimeter of the "sundial's" shadow. The sketcher should mark each tracing with the time.
7. At the end of the day, there is a pattern of shadows that is close to a sundial.

EXTENSIONS

—If you are studying seasons, do this activity using a very large piece of paper. Trace the shadows on to the paper, and mark the date. At the beginning of each season, make another sundial. Compare the sundials and have the class find reasons for the differences!

—Have the class create their own versions of a sundial.

—Find a copy of the book *The Great Sundial Cutout Book* by Robert Adzema and Mablen Jones (Hawthorn/Dutton, New York, 1978). This book has the history of sundials, and it provides patterns by which the students can create very different, delightful sundials. The book has patterns for fourteen sundials that students can construct. The directions are clear and the reasons why each sundial works are given. The book is a treasure for anyone studying sundials. It shows how art and science can work together with wondrous results.

MAKE YOUR CLASSROOM INTO A CAMERA OBSCURA

INTRODUCTION

When studying light, cameras, the human eye, or anything else that might fit, why not turn your classroom into a giant camera obscura? The camera obscura, the primative beginnings of modern photography, demonstrates how our eye works, as well as how cameras work.

PROCEDURE

1. Collect cardboard boxes or other heavy material. Perhaps the class could save posters used in other classes, if boxes aren't available. Remember to use recycled materials. You need to always set a good example for the class.

2. Have the class estimate when they think enough materials have been collected to cover the windows and doors of the class to permit no light to enter the room from outside sources.

3. Before and on the day you turn the classroom into a camera, tell the folks in the office that you are undertaking this project. Fire drills or other interruptions can be bothersome.

4. Cover the windows first. Use tape to secure the flattened cardboard. Tape over any holes in the cardboard. Next, tape cardboard over any interior windows. Seal around the door by extending cardboard over the edge of the door. DO NOT SEAL THE DOOR CLOSED; IT MUST BE AVAILABLE AS AN EXIT AT ALL TIMES!

5. Now you are ready to test for darkness. Turn off the lights. Notice light leaks, and mark them. Turn the lights back on, and seal the leaks. Continue this process until all light leaks have been sealed.

6. Using a large darning needle, make a small hole in one of the pieces of cardboard that covers the windows.

7. Take the portable movie screen and move it back and forth until the light from the hole focuses on the screen.

8. If necessary, enlarge the hole until the class can see the upside-down image of whatever is outside the classroom. (You might need to swap rooms with someone who has a good "view" if you don't have anything outside of your window!)

9. Ask the class to speculate what will happen if the hole is enlarged even more. When student-suggested possibilities have been discussed, ask the class to predict which of the possibilities, if any, will happen.

   Enlarge the hole, and ask the class to notice what has happened to the image. Keep enlarging the hole until the image is lost. Have the class speculate as to why the image is sharpest with the smallest hole, and why the image was eventually lost.

10. Now don't be hasty at this point. The class will be fascinated by this phenomenon. Don't tell them why things work the way they do. You might want to take them to the library to do their own research or conduct further experiments. If you give the class the answers right away, you deprive the students of the joy of discovering the answer for themselves. They'll be motivated and they'll try to find answers; let them.

11. Allow a day or two for the students to discover answers. Provide time for any student who wishes to explain the phenomenon to the class. Make sure that explanations are clear and accurate. As a final review, you should sum up the whole project. If some explanations have been foggy or not quite accurate, the teacher might offer a clear, accurate explanation.

EXTENSIONS

—Provide the class with instructions on how to make a pin hole camera, and allow the class to experiment with the completed product.

—Research and discuss optical illusions. Ask each member of the class to find one optical illusion, and share it with the class (Optical Illusion Day!).

—Investigate how animals see:

1. Have the class draw pictures of familiar objects as if they were observed by a bee, an ant, or a dragonfly. (Those compound eyes do make a difference!)

2. Ask one half of the class to draw a fly as if they were orb web-weaving spiders. Ask the other half to draw a fly as if they were jumping spiders. (Jumping spiders have very good eyesight, orb web weavers don't.)

3. Request that the class research the eyesight of hawks and eagles. They see very small prey from great heights. How do they do that?

—Ask the class to think about animal camouflage. What do the animals that use camouflage do? Why is it effective? Is mimicry a form of camouflage?

A good book that deals with sight is *How Animals See Other Visions Of Our World* by Sandra Sinclair (Croom Helm Ltd., 1985).

SCIENCE QUESTION OF THE WEEK

INTRODUCTION

A fun way to encourage intellectual curiosity is to create a bulletin board that asks a new, thought-provoking question at the beginning of each week. The students can guess at the answer all week, but no answer is denied or confirmed until the last day of the week.

The whole concept for this activity came about when I was given a bunch of old *Smithsonian* magazines. As I was leafing through them, a picture of two people caught my eye. They were paddling a dugout canoe down a stream, and they both had masks on the backs of their heads. I stared at the photo for a long time, but couldn't come up with a reasonable explanation for such behavior. When I read the article to find the answer, I was flabbergasted, and decided to challenge my students to find the answer.

I created the first poster and put it on a bulletin board on a Monday. By Friday the guesses were flying fast and furious. After they came up with the answer, (YES, they were able to come up with it!) they clamored for more. It had been fun and non-threatening for all of the students! The highlight of most Fridays is the answer to the "Question of the Week!" Try it...the kids will love it!

Oh, about the natives who were wearing masks on the backs of their heads...the reason they did was that tigers who were endangered were now making a comeback in their land. Tigers will attack and kill people, BUT tigers usually attack from the rear. Since these people have two fronts, (and no rear) the tigers don't tend to attack them! The *Smithsonian* magazine which featured this photo was Volume 13, Number 11.

OVERVIEW

Students develop answers to each weekly question that is posted on the bulletin board. The project continues throughout the year.

PROCEDURE

1. Find appropriate pictures from various educational magazines such as:
   The Smithsonian
   Natural History
   National Geographic
   Scientific American
   Science
   Audubon
   Popular Science
2. After a photo or drawing has been selected, decide on an appropriate question. Make sure that the answer can be found through research on logical thought.

3. Mount the picture on a large piece of paper, and have it laminated.

Since my school year is 36 weeks long, one project that I undertake each summer is to create a series of 36 posters that ask the "Question of the Week." I also keep a notebook with the answers to the question of the week.

Some of the posters have included the following:

—Electron scanning microscope photos of the skin of animals. The students had to guess which animals' skins were pictured.

—A photo of a door to a 1880's subway car that had been abandoned. The poster states, "This was discovered in 1912. What is it? What did it do?"

—A photo of two men; one man is juggling lemons and limes. The question: "Are these guys REALLY juggling? If not, how are they able to fake it? If so, which way are the lemons and limes moving? Clockwise or counterclockwise? How do you know?"

—A photo of leaves frozen under water. The question: "What is this?"

—A photo of mouse tracks that end abruptly at an imprint of wings in the snow. The question: "What story does this picture tell?"

—A sketch of a helicopter from Leonardo da Vinci's notebook. The question: "What is this? What natural things influenced this design?"

—A photo of the SR-71 Blackbird. (A very fast military airplane) "What is this? Why is it painted black? How does its shape help it accomplish its function?"

—A photo of a tiger jumping into a river. "Why is this tiger doing this?"

—A photo of a man rappelling down a building. "Is he climbing or descending? How do you know? Any suggestions as to why he's doing this?"

■ WATER CLEARING DEVICES ■

INTRODUCTION

When studying the water resource or water pollution, students should learn how water can be cleaned. Depending on the pollutant, different methods need to be employed. A good exercise for students is to clean water that has dirt mixed in it as a suspension. Students need to develop a theory of how to clean the water, predict their results, use trial and error in testing, adapt their device and finally produce a device that works.

OVERVIEW

Students create water clearing devices that remove dirt from water. The devices need to meet the standards of time, cost, efficiency and effectiveness.

PROCEDURE

NOTE: This is an activity that just removes large particles from water. The devices will probably not be able to remove dissolved salts, microscopic plants and animals, or other pollutants. Under no circumstances should students be allowed to drink the water that has been purified. (See EXTENSIONS for water that the class can drink)

1. Introduce the project by handing each student the rules of the contest.

   —Students will create a device that attempts to remove 10 grams of dirt from 250 ml of water in 5 minutes.

   —The device must return at least 125 ml of water to the collecting jar.

   —No more than $3.00 can be spent on materials for this project. Students who spend no money by using all recycled materials will receive bonus points on their score sheets.

*NOTE: IF THE STUDENTS HAVE NO ABILITY TO PURCHASE MATERIALS SIMPLY DELETE THE COST LIMIT SECTION AND REQUIRE THAT ALL MATERIALS SHOULD BE RECYCLED.

   —Each device will be rated by its ability to clean the dirt from the water.

WATER CLARITY RATING SCALE

clear –10
mostly clear – 8
slightly dirty – 6
dirty – 4
very dirty – 2
same as when it went in – 0

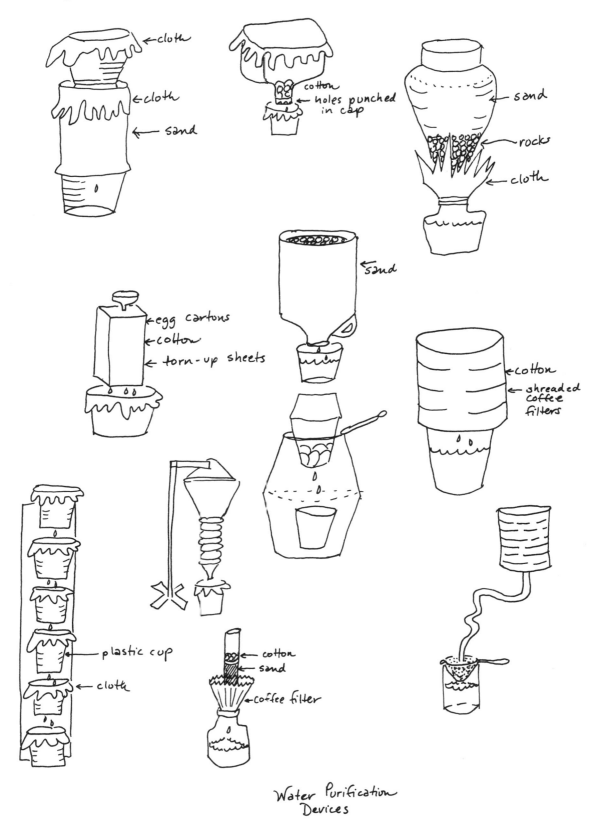

Water Purification
Devices

Name_____   Date_____

WONDROUS WAYS TO CLEAN WATER · CONTEST RULES

You are about to embark on an unforgettable adventure. You will act somewhat like a magician: YOU WILL REMOVE DIRT FROM WATER! But no hocus-pocus is needed; you can allow everyone to see how you do it. Just follow the rules, think hard and create a great device, add your own flair to the demonstration, and presto! clean water.

RULES

You will create a device that will clean 10 grams of dirt from 250 ml of water in 5 minutes. The device must return at least 125 ml of water to the collecting jar.

You may spend up to $3.00 for materials, but if you spend no money *and* use all recycled materials, you will receive bonus points.

The water will be rated according to the following scale:

WATER CLARITY RATING SCALE
clear – 10
mostly clear – 8
slightly dirty – 6
dirty – 4
very dirty – 2
same as when it went in – 0

You may seek help from your parents or anyone else as long as you are the one who does most of the work.

This project is due on_____.

Written plan and sketch reviewed, okayed for construction.

_____   _____teacher's signature

© 1990 by The Center for Applied Research in Education

WONDROUS WAYS TO CLEAN WATER—LAB RECORD SHEET

Student	Materials Used	Effective?	Met all Qualifications?	Water Rating

Name _____ Date _____

WATER CLEARING DEVICES—TEACHER RECORDS

Student	Time	Clarity	Creativity	Materials Used	Effective?

1. Distribute Lab Record Sheet

2. Allow the students to work individually or in small groups.

3. If students need help in designing their devices, provide guidance, but do not tell them how to proceed. Before students begin construction, they should have written plans with sketches that detail the design of the device.

4. On testing day, appoint one student to be the "official timer." Another student should be asked to be the "official water/dirt measurer." Write the rating scale on the board.
   After each device has been tested, allow all students to have input to determine the rating of the filtered water.

5. List what worked and what didn't work on the board.

6. Students keep a lab record sheet of each device tested. The lab sheet should include the name of the student, what materials the device was made from, the rating the filtered water received, and whether or not the device met all the qualifications.

7. When all the students have tested their devices, have the class look over their lab sheets and decide which materials seemed to work best. Also have the class suggest other factors that helped to determine the outcome (craftmanship, design, etc.)

8. Award ribbons to all students who deserve them (for good design, effective design, creative design, and so on.)

9. Have the students evaluate the project the day after all the devices have been tested. Make sure to review all of the factors that made effective devices. Offer constructive criticism for the ones that didn't work.

EXTENSIONS

—Read Joanna Cole's *The Magic School Bus at the Waterworks* to the class. In the story, the class travels through the water cycle into a water purification plant. Alum is added to the water to make the dirt clump together and fall to the bottom of a tank.

If none of the students added alum to remove the dirt from the water in the water activity, have the class set up an experiment that uses alum to clear water. (Alum can be purchased in the spice department of a supermarket or at a drug store.)

—Have the class generate ideas for devices to remove other pollutants from water (heavy metals, poisons, municipal wastes, and so on.)

—Create a REAL water purification device that is slow, but truly effective. The class can construct a water still.

A WATER STILL

1. Necessary materials are a large pan, some clear plastic wrap, and a clean, smaller pan that will hold 1 liter of water.

2. Take 1 liter of water and stir dirt into it.

3. Ask the class to think of a method to clear the water for drinking purposes. (Remind them of the water purification project where the water only removed solids and left most dissolved and microscopic things.)

4. Tell the class that there is a way to make the water pure enough to drink. The method is one that people have used for centuries to obtain clean drinking water and is still used by people throughout the world.

5. Take the large pan and put the dirty water in it.

6. Put the clean small pan in the center of the large pan. Make sure that the sides of the smaller pan are well below the sides of the large pan. If the small pan won't stay in place, weigh it down by putting something that is clean inside it. Make sure that whatever you use to weigh down the small pan won't affect the clean water.

7. Seal the top of the large pan with the clear plastic wrap. Place a small stone in the center of the plastic wrap top. Make sure that the plastic wrap does not touch the small pan.

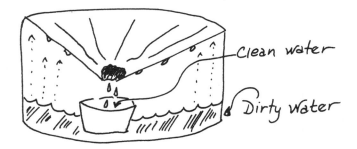

8. Place the large pan in the sunlight.

9. Ask the class to speculate how the water cleaning device will work. Also ask how long they think it will take.

10. When water is in the inside pan, open the still, and allow the class to see the clean water. It is drinkable!

11. Ask the class how the device can be adapted to survival situations. (Plants, cacti, dirty water, etc. can be in the large pan.) The water will still evaporate, and provide clean, safe drinking water. This is how our Earth's water cycle works...except in miniature! If your curriculum includes the water cycle, why not use the Water Still activity as a kick off point?

THE BIG EVENT

INTRODUCTION

Use this activity as either a review or a problem-solving competition. Either way, the class comes alive as they work in small groups attempting to answer the questions before the buzzer sounds!

OVERVIEW

The "Big Event" is a round robin activity in which small groups of students work together to solve a series of science problems within a set period of time. Each group starts at a different station. When time has elapsed, the group moves on to the next station and so on. The group keeps moving until it has been to each station.

PROCEDURE

1. Duplicate the problem cards and answer sheets. Laminate the cards so they will be reusable. Make one answer sheet for each group participating in the "Big Event."

2. If you wish, make your own cards. This activity lends itself to the review of material covered in class, especially if there is a great deal of material. Don't forget to make answer sheets to go with your questions!

3. The event can be conducted outdoors or indoors. I prefer to do it outdoors, since it seems to make it more special for the students when they are outdoors.

4. A few days prior to the "Big Event," ask the class to divide into groups of three or four. Tell them what they will need to study to prepare for the "Big Event" if this is used as a review. If the task cards are being used, make up a "sample problem" similar to one of the cards, and let the groups attempt to solve it. Ask the groups to plan their strategies for problem solving.

5. The number of groups will determine how many stations are needed. Decide how much time will be allotted to each station. If you feel that there should be more time, plan to do the activity on two consecutive days.

6. When you begin, have a unique means of signaling that time has elapsed, use a whistle, boat horn, buzzer or whatever...you can even make the noise yourself!

7. Announce the results of the "Big Event" as soon as possible.

8. Discuss each problem, and the possible solutions with the class.

MATERIALS NEEDED FOR THE TASK CARDS

A: A piece of string about 1 meter long.

B: One pocket loupe for each member of the group.

C: No supplies needed.

D: Two # 10 cans each half filled with water. One can is painted with flat black paint. Both cans should be in direct sunlight. They should be in the sun at least one hour before the activity.
1 thermometer.

E: No supplies needed.

F: No supplies needed.

G: No supplies needed.

H: No supplies needed.

MEASURING...

- Find (but don't pick) ten objects that are the same length as the string.
- Find five objects that are half the length of the string.
- Find one object that is ten times the length of the string.

A

USING A POCKET LOUPE...

FIND

OBJECTS THAT HAVE THE SAME

PATTERN

AS THESE:

1   2   3   4   5   **B**

ANT HILL

Why do the tunnels that lead from the central tunnel usually lead upward?

Name three different jobs that ants have.
How do ants communicate with one another? C

Measure the temperature in both cans.
Which has the higher temperature?
How much higher is it?
Please explain WHY one is higher than the other.

D

SEEDS

Name 10 different seeds.

List them in order from smallest to largest.

E

MATCH the seed and the leaf.

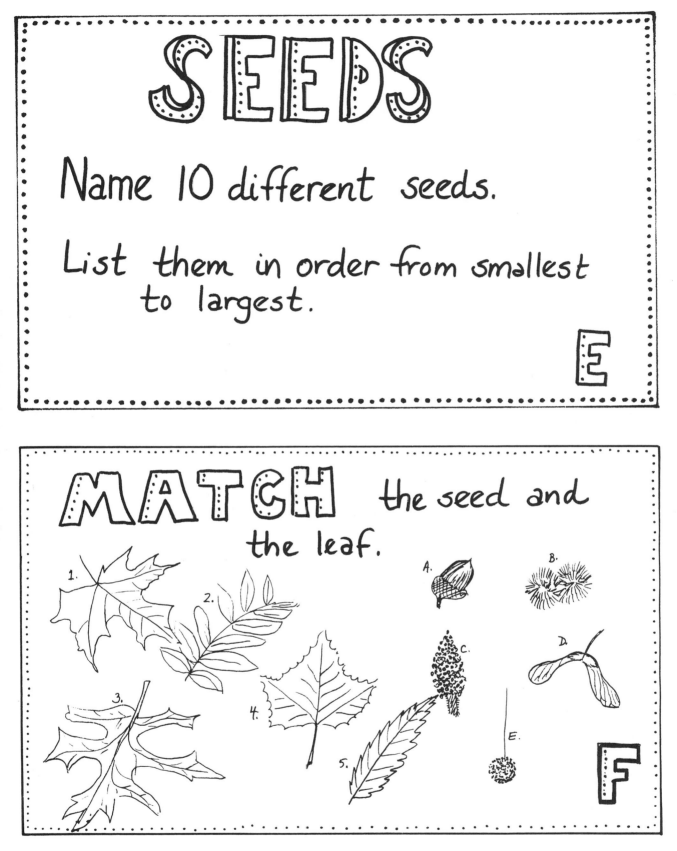

F

Why don't spiders get caught in their own webs?

G

Mold and bacteria aren't always bad. Please think of three ways that they are very useful to our world.

H

Name_____ Date_____

Group Members _____

THE BIG EVENT ANSWER SHEET

Card A:

1. _____   6. _____

2. _____   7. _____

3. _____   8. _____

4. _____   9. _____

5. _____   10. _____

1. _____

2. _____

3. _____

4. _____

5. _____

Card B:

1. _____

2. _____

3. _____

4. _____

5. _____

Card C: _____

_____

1. _____ 2. _____ 3. _____

_____

_____

THE BIG EVENT ANSWER SHEET, PAGE 2

Card D: Can 1 _____

Can 2 _____

_____

Card E:

1. _____	1. _____
2. _____	2. _____
3. _____	3. _____
4. _____	4. _____
5. _____	5. _____
6. _____	6. _____
7. _____	7. _____
8. _____	8. _____
9. _____	9. _____
10. _____	10. _____

Card F:

Leaf 1. _____

Leaf 2. _____

Leaf 3. _____

Leaf 4. _____

Leaf 5. _____

Card G: _____

_____

Card H: 1. _____

2. _____

3. _____

TESTING THE CORIOLIS EFFECT

The Coriolis effect is the result of an object moving freely over a moving surface. Since the Earth is rotating on its axis and revolving around the sun, it is a moving surface. The air and water on the Earth are objects that move freely over the Earth's surface. So, the air and water are affected by the movement of the Earth. In the northern hemisphere, because of this movement, an object tends to move to the right. In the southern hemisphere, an object tends to move to the left.

When we study weather and oceans, one of the factors that we need to consider is that the water and air of the Earth are affected by its rotation and revolution. Air and water currents in the northern hemisphere tend to be deflected in a counterclockwise direction. In the southern hemisphere, they tend to be deflected in a clockwise direction.

One way to have the class understand the idea of the Coriolis effect might be to put a large pan of water on a table. Float a small cork on the surface of the water. Mark a spot at the edge of the pan where the cork is going to bump the edge. Give the cork a gentle push toward the spot, and have the class note that it did indeed go where it was expected to go. Now point the cork at the spot once again, but this time as you push the cork toward the edge, ask two or three students to gently turn the table in a circular motion. Is it still going to hit the same spot? Why doesn't the cork land in the same spot? Have the class observe the water in the pan. Is the water moving? In what direction is it moving? Does the direction of the water in the pan have anything to do with the cork and the place the cork landed?

If you have a merry-go-round nearby, another good illustration of the way the Coriolis effect works is to ask two students to sit on opposite sides of the merry-go-round and throw a ball to one another while it is still. Then they should do the same thing while the merry-go round is moving. It is a fact that the ball is still going to the same spot, it's the person on the merry-go-round who has moved!

An interesting note found in an article about the Coriolis effect in the February 1983 issue of *Smithsonian*, Alan Linn mentions that the World War I cannon, Big Bertha, fired shells at Paris from a distance of 76 miles. The shell took three minutes to get from the cannon to Paris. In that time Paris rotated 1 mile, so the shells missed Paris by a mile!

OVERVIEW

Students attempt to discover whether or not the Coriolis effect is demonstrated by the whirlpools that develop as bathtubs drain.

INTRODUCTION

The Coriolis effect, that invisible result of the earth's movement, has often been claimed to demonstrate itself by the whirlpool which appears as water is drained from a bathtub. But, if you ask the class to test this theory, does the whirlpool always move counterclockwise? The answer is a resounding no—bathtub whirlpools don't always move counterclockwise. Does that mean that the Coriolis effect is a lie? Have the class try to reason things out. Testing theories as scientists do is a great way to get the class thinking.

This is a good lesson to undertake prior to a study of weather, since the Coriolis effect does play a part in the formation of high and low pressure systems, as well as ocean and air currents.

PROCEDURE

1. Introduce the concept of the Coriolis effect to the class. (See the Introduction of this section.)
2. Tell the students that some people claim that the whirlpool in a draining bathtub demonstrates the Coriolis effect. Have the class set up an experiment which will determine whether or not the whirlpool always moves in a counterclockwise direction. The Coriolis effect worksheet at the end of this section will help to set up the experiment.
3. Have the class research the whirlpools. They will discover that they do not always move counterclockwise...sometimes they move clockwise, and sometimes the whirlpool changes direction midway through the tub being drained!
4. Ask the class what explanations they have for this!

NOTE: According to most experts, the reasons for the effect not always applying to the draining bathtub are as follows:

> residual motion from the tub being filled
> air movement in the room
> temperature differences in the room
> irregularities in the shape of the drain

In the article about the Coriolis effect in the February 1983 issue of *Smithsonian*, Alan Linn reported that Ascher H. Shapiro, of the Massachussetts Institute of Technology, discovered that in a bathtub located in the middle latitudes the Coriolis force is about 30 million times weaker than the force of gravity. Dr. Shapiro did build a special tub and tested the Coriolis effect. With all of the other factors removed, the tub did always drain in a counterclockwise direction.

5. By now the class should feel pretty confident about the dynamics of bathtub whirlpools. So here is the opportunity to discuss the things that are effected by the Coriolis effect: weather systems, ocean currents, free swinging pendulums, and missiles.

Name_____ Date_____

TESTING THEORIES...IS THE WHIRLPOOL
IN THE BATHTUB AN EXAMPLE OF THE

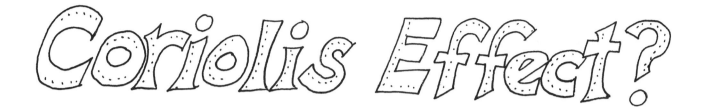

Trial #	Place: Bathtub, Sink	Direction of Whirlpool (clockwise or counterclockwise)

Remember: Trials should be observed after the water has been used for a good reason. You shouldn't just fill the tub with water to let it out...take the bath first. Offer to wash the dishes in the sink so you can observe the whirlpool when you're finished. PLEASE DON'T WASTE CLEAN WATER!

◼◼◼◼◼ THE GREAT ICE CUBE MELT ◼◼◼◼◼

INTRODUCTION

Don't just talk about insulation and insulators, have the kids find out for themselves what works and what doesn't. This is an activity that generates a great deal of excitement and enthusiasm in the classroom.

OVERVIEW

Students design and create containers that will keep one standard sized ice cube in its solid form for a set period of time. The winner is the person who creates the container that keeps the ice cube solid for the longest period of time. After the actual "Great Ice Cube Melt" students analyze what worked and what didn't.

PROCEDURE

1. About a week before you begin, construct a large sign or banner in multi-colored letters which announces that:

THE GREAT ICE CUBE MELT IS COMING SOON!

2. When students ask about the sign, tell them that it is true, but keep them in suspense. Say no more than "Yes, the sign is correct." You might even wish to add another smaller sign which counts down the days until you announce what it is.

3. On the day that you begin this project, start with a class discussion. Have the students determine which materials they feel will act as insulators and which will act as conductors.

4. Announce that each student will have the opportunity to test his/her own theory, since all students will participate in "The Great Ice Cube Melt."

5. The rules are simple. Students must design and construct a container of the materials that they think will keep an ice cube from melting. The ice cube that lasts longest is the winner! You may wish to set container size limits, and insist that the students use recycled materials only. (See the RULES hand-out for more details.)

6. On the day of the GREAT ICE CUBE MELT, have several older students, aides, parent volunteers or teachers available for the check in. All containers must be measured and verified to insure that they are within the rules.

7. Insert a standard sized ice cube into each container. (You determine what the standard size is)

8. Have a table, floor or counter top where all containers will stay. Make sure that they aren't near a heat source, a sunny window or any other variable that might

RULES FOR THE GREAT ICE CUBE MELT

1. Students should use recycled materials wherever possible.

2. The most money that can be spent on this project is $2.00.

3. Any container over 6 inches by 6 inches by 6 inches will be disqualified.

4. Containers or any portion of the container may not be frozen at any time prior to the competition.

5. Only one ice cube will be allowed per container.

6. All designs must allow for the inspection of the ice cube at various time intervals to determine the status of the cube.

7. The container may *not* be something which has been already created as an insulator such as an insulated picnic cooler. It must be each students original design.

8. Parents may assist students, but the project MUST be mostly student work.

9. Containers may not be plugged into electrical outlets or powered by batteries, generators or any other power-supplying device.

BE CREATIVE, PLAY WITHIN THE RULES, AND GOOD LUCK!

make the contest invalid. All containers should be evenly spaced, and experience the same conditions.

9. Check the containers on a regular basis. You should inspect the ice cubes at hour or hour-and-a-half intervals. Any container that has allowed its ice cube to melt should be moved to an area for non winning entries. Each container should be marked with the time that it was removed from the competition.

10. At the end of the school day, check all remaining containers. At this point you have several options as to how the activity is ended.

—If any ice cubes are still quite large, you may wish to allow those containers to remain overnight to see whether any container will keep its ice cube overnight.

—Or you may wish to declare all those cubes who have survived the winners.

—You may also choose to measure the surviving ice cubes and the ice cube with the largest size may be declared the winner.

—You may choose to combine any of the above.

11. Ribbons are a good reward for the winners. Create ribbons and attach them to the winning entries.

12. The next day in class have each student explain his container and how it worked. Keep a list of what worked and what didn't on a chalkboard or on a large piece of poster paper.

13. Compare the performance of the different insulators, and discuss the reasons for the effectiveness of the different entries.

EXTENSIONS

1. You may wish to have the students design houses for the tundra or the tropics that keep the interior temperatures comfortable.

2. You may research how igloos are made and how they work and then, as a class, construct one.

3. Invite a local house builder to speak to the class about the materials and methods used to make homes more energy efficient.

4. Have the class brainstorm how they think boiling water could be kept the warmest for the longest period of time.

RECYCLING

■ RECYCLED NEEDS CHART ■

INTRODUCTION

Since recycled materials are frequently used in classrooms, an organized method of acquiring those materials helps! This chart, which is a permanent display in the classroom, lists the materials that are needed for upcoming lessons and activities. Students can also place requests for items on the board.

OVERVIEW

Using a large piece of oaktag or other heavy paper, create a chart that is slotted. When items are needed for lessons in the near future, they are posted on the board. When the need is filled, that card is removed from the board.

PROCEDURE

1. Find a large piece of cardboard or oaktag.
2. Using a ruler and matte knife, cut a series of one inch vertical slits in the board.
3. Cut pieces of scrap paper into rectangles that are one inch by seven inches.
4. When a recycled item is needed, place the name of the item on one of the rectangles, and slip the paper between the slits of the cardboard.
5. As the needs are filled, remove the paper from the board so there is room for other requests.

THE STORY OF MY ALUMINUM CAN

The time has come for all of us to stop throwing away our valuable, finite resources. The classroom is a perfect place to teach young people the importance of recycling. Even though creating a scrap paper pile for paper only used on one side is a small thing, it is important to show our students that it does matter that they recycle. It is important for all of us to recycle!

OVERVIEW

Students create stories about the adventures of an aluminum can as it was recycled into different products.

PROCEDURE

1. Have each student bring in an aluminum soda can. Make sure that it has been rinsed out so that it doesn't smell.

NOTE: You may prefer to save up your own soda cans and then provide one for each student when you do this activity. If you do have the children bring in their own cans, discourage them from bringing in alcoholic beverage cans. It really is hard to explain to a visiting parent why the kids all have beer cans on their desks!

2. With the kids, brainstorm all of the things that they can think of that are made from aluminum. Put the names of the aluminum products all over the board as they are suggested. Two suggestions:

   —First, use colored chalk; kids love it! (Just make sure that it is the kind of colored chalk that is made for blackboards.)

   —Second, have the kids who make each suggestion write it on the board themselves. It tends to be easier for the teacher to keep the flow of ideas going, rather than getting bogged down in writing and having children waiting!

3. After the students have no more ideas, (and it might take a LONG time for that to happen!) or the board is totally filled, ask the class to look at all of the things that are made of aluminum.

4. You might want to point out that aluminum is quite readily recycled. As a matter of fact, it takes 95 percent LESS energy to recycle aluminum than it takes to dig the bauxite from the ground, and process it into new aluminum. So recycling aluminum not only saves it from taking up space in the landfill, it saves energy as well!

5. Ask each student to place the aluminum can on his/her desk. Students should have a piece of paper and pencil ready to use.

6. Have each student name his/her can.

7. After suitable names have been found for every can, announce that it has been recycled many, many times. Ask the students to imagine the things that their can might have been and then to write a story about the "Adventure of My Aluminum Can." You probably will need to ask the students to name a fixed number of recyclings for their can. Three or four recyclings should do fine for a reasonable story.

You might have to remind the students that the story needs to flow, and they must find ways to get the aluminum to the recycling center so that it can be changed into a new item. Aluminum doesn't magically recycle itself; people need to get it to the recycling center. The use of transitional paragraphs can be stressed if this is being done at upper grade levels.

EXTENSIONS AND SUGGESTIONS

1. If you are dealing with very young students, you may wish to have them draw the "Adventures of My Aluminum Can." When the stories are completed, have the students share them with one another.

2. You may wish to have the class create a collective story about one can that you display at the front of the room.

3. Have the students create a collage of pictures cut from old magazines. The pictures should be things that are made of aluminum. Display each student's collage with the aluminum can in front of it. The whole thing might be titled: RALPH THE ALUMINUM CAN—THIS IS YOUR LIFE.

4. Give the students a large piece of paper. If possible, use the back of a poster that has something already on the other side. Have them draw the outline of a huge can that takes up most of the paper. Ask the students to draw pictures of things that are made of aluminum within the outline.

5. The possibilities are unlimited...use your imagination! You might have the art teacher help you create giant can costumes for the students to put on skits about the things aluminum cans may be turned into.

It is important to teach by example. So, when you have finished, please don't forget to recycle the cans that you have used for the activity.

■ NATURE RECYCLES TOO ■

INTRODUCTION

In the interrelationship of all living things, how nature itself recycles is amazingly elegant: deciduous trees drop their leaves, which provide food for worms, insects, fungi and bacteria, that in turn help to break down the leaves, which enrich the soil so that plants have better soil to grow in!

To make this cycle come alive for children, one activity that shows graphically how fungus and bacteria break down leaves is WINDOW ON A DECOMPOSING LEAF. It follows logically that after students have watched the leaves become good soil, they should then find seeds in foods to plant in their newly-enriched soil, and so we come to the second activity, LEAVES TO HELP SEEDS.

WINDOW ON A DECOMPOSING LEAF

OVERVIEW

These activities focus on the process by which nature recycles itself, yet incorporated in the activities is scientific method (creating theories, predicting outcomes, creating a model, observing the process, determining results.) Students are active in the experiments, and compare and share their results with others. Aside from learning how nature recycles things, students discover what seeds look like, where they come from, what a specific plant looks like as it grows from a seed, and that different seeds produce different-looking plants.

PROCEDURE

1. This activity is an on-going one. The Window on the Leaf World activity takes at least six weeks, but the actual class time spent on the activity is only four class periods during that time frame.

2. Gather the necessary materials before you begin this activity. You'll need:

   one 2 liter soda container for each student

   enough soil so that each container can be two-thirds filled. The soil should be good, fertile soil.

   paper and colored pencils, crayons, or markers for the students to make their sketches.

3. Ask the students to bring in a number of leaves that have fallen from trees.

4. In a class discussion, you may wish to have students point out how the leaves are different from one another. (Color, size, shape, margin outline, stem, brittleness, etc.) It isn't necessary for the students to be able to identify each of the leaves that they have brought in, but they may wish to. *Peterson's Field Guide to North*

American Trees or the *Audubon Field Guide to North American Trees* are both good for students' research efforts since both are relatively easy to use.

5. Ask the students what will happen to the leaves if they put them outside. Develop as many theories as possible about what happens to leaves after they fall. (Burn, blow away, fall into the sea, go to leaf heaven, disintegrate, etc.)

6. Have each of the students predict which of the theories is correct. You may wish to create a chart which records each student's prediction using words or possibly symbols for each theory.

7. Before distributing the 2-liter bottles to each student, cut off the top of the bottle, so that it resembles a tall cylinder. Who does the actual plastic-cutting depends on the grade level at which this activity is being used. Sixth graders should be able to handle the actual cutting (with supervision), but in any event try to have it done before the lesson begins.

8. To create the window on the leaf world container, have each student put some soil in the bottom of the container. It should reach to about 1 inch above the opaque bottom. Next, have the students set aside one leaf for observing; the rest should be crumpled and put into the container. Add an inch or so more soil on top of the crumpled leaves.

9. Have the students place their reserved leaf against the inside of the container and carefully add soil to the container so that the whole leaf is still visible against the side.

10. Have each student draw his/her leaf as they see it through the plastic. Point out that it doesn't have to be a perfect drawing, but it should have a shape and color similar to the real leaf in the container.

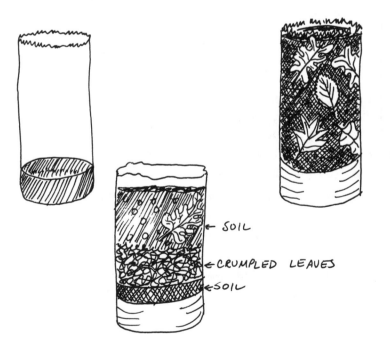
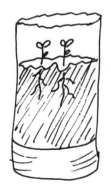

11. Place the picture near the container or somewhere where students can have easy access to the drawing. A file folder may be a good place to store the drawings.

12. Add a little water to the container as the soil dries out, but try not to flood the containers. If you wish, you might have the children add water to the containers on days that it rains, since the experiment is an attempt to duplicate what happens to leaves in the real world! If you choose not to duplicate the rains, add water every three or four days. Bacteria and fungi need water to grow.

NOTE: If you or any of the students has allergies to mold, cover each container with plastic wrap and secure with a rubber band.

13. Each day, observe the leaves in the containers, and point out whenever a change in one of the leaves has occurred (white "stuff" growing on it, black "stuff," color disappearing, shriveling up, mushrooms growing on it, whatever.)

14. After two weeks, ask the students to draw the leaves again and compare them with the original drawing. How have the leaves changed? What could be causing these changes? What is the "stuff" growing on the leaves?

15. Place the second drawing with the first and water as before.

16. After four weeks, have the students draw the leaves again. Discuss the changes as before.

17. At the end of six weeks, have the students draw a final picture of the leaf. Discuss the things that have changed the leaves.

EXTENSIONS

1. You may wish to have the students bring in other items to be placed in their containers to see the ways that different things break down. Compare the drawings of the leaf project to see if similar things work on the apple cores, peach pits, lettuce, potatoes, or whatever.

2. Or ask students to save one edible thing from their lunch and place that thing in the container and compare all of the various foods as they decompose.

RESOURCES

Two great trade books that might be used with this or any other activity that focuses on trees and the life cycles of trees are:

The Fall of Freddie the Leaf, by Leo Buscaglia. New York: Charles B. Slack, Inc., 1982.

Oak and Company, by Richard Mabey. New York: Greenwillow Books, 1983.

Both are informative, well-written books that students of all ages love to listen to. Most people love to hear a good story. Don't feel that your students are "too old" for picture books. Success is in how you, the teacher, handle the reading. It CAN be done at any grade level!

   If your school library doesn't have these books, try your local public library. If they don't have them, ask if they will try to locate them through an inter-library loan sevice. They are both worth the effort!

■■■■■■ LEAVES TO HELP SEEDS GROW ■■■■■■

INTRODUCTION

Tie the recycling activities together! Build one activity so that you utilize the activity before tying them all into a neat package that is fun and rewarding.

OVERVIEW

Students take advantage of the rich soil that they have created in the "Window on a Decomposing Leaf" activity. They identify the seed of familiar as well as unfamiliar fruits and vegetables, play a memory game, plant their seeds and record their growth.

PROCEDURE

1. Gather familiar and unfamiliar fruits and vegetables. You should include apples, peaches, plums, kiwis, pomegranates, oranges, avocados, tomatoes, green peppers, grapefruits, grapes, bananas, squash, or pumpkins.

If your school budget is limited, ask each student to bring in one of the fruits or veggies!

2. Discuss seeds with the students.

3. After each of the students has a fruit or vegetable, have them discover the seed in their fruit/vegetable.

4. Ask the students to identify the seed of the item that they have. After students have discovered the seed in their fruit/vegetable, have them report to the class just where they found their seed, and show the class what it looks like. As each student shows his/her seed to the class, have each person leave his/her seed on a piece of construction paper (preferably used on one side already) in front of the room.

5. Play the MEMORY GAME. (See the box)

6. When the game is over, the seeds need to be planted. Have the students plant a few of their seeds in the container they used for the leaf decomposition activity.

7. Ask the students why plants make seeds. Discuss plant life cycles.

THE MEMORY GAME

1. When everyone has finished showing their seeds, draw a large circle around each seed, and sequentially number each circle.

2. Ask the class to divide into groups of two or three. Each group needs to find a piece of scrap paper, with lines, and number the lines with the same number as there are circles. It's time to play the Memory Game!

3. Each group must identify as many of the seeds as possible. The group might identify the seed structure as it identifies the seed.

4. The group that correctly identifies the most number of seeds is declared the winner!

8. After two or three weeks, discuss with the class the progress of the seeds in the containers. If there are enough plants visible, have the students sketch them. If a student doesn't have a growing plant in his/her container, he/she might share with another student. If necessary, plant commercially packaged seeds in the containers.

9. Make this an ongoing activity. Have the students note the growth of their plants. Measurements such as height of the plant and the number of leaves that it has might be used for scientific record keeping.

SUGGESTIONS

Not all classrooms are good for growing plants. Some have north-facing windows, or no windows at all! If that is the case, the class can still start seeds in the classroom, and then take the plants home after two or three weeks. If the students want their plants to remain at school, perhaps there is a good window in the office, or in one of the other classrooms. Look around, move some furniture if necessary, but don't give up. Kids love growing things!

When growing plants for classroom experiments, a great plant to use is the green bean! The plant produces beans even in classrooms. When it flowers, and produces beans, the kids just love it! When the bean plant is producing, a bean pod can be offered a as reward. The plant, in the students' care, usually flourishes as long as the tendency to over-water it is curbed. Adding some water-soluble plant food to the bean plant once a week really makes a difference too. If you wish, have the class experiment with the fertilizer. Create one group of plants that is fertilized every week and one group that gets no fertilizer. Have the students observe the differences! Ask the class to develop other experiments for the plants.

■■■■■■■■ THE RECYCLED BAND ■■■■■■■■

INTRODUCTION

Making musical instruments from recycled cans, bottles, containers, and whatever is a fun way to point out the merits of trash, and has the class involved in stretching their imaginations at the same time. This activity is great to use when you're studying sound!

OVERVIEW

Students make instruments from recycled materials. They discover the properties of sound as they make music with the instruments that they have created.

PROCEDURE

1. During a class discussion, ask the students if they feel that it might be possible to create musical instruments from recycled products.
2. Brainstorm the possible things that might be used for such a project. Try to not name specific instruments that can be made; rather, try to brainstorm all sorts of things that people normally throw away that have potential for making musical instruments.
3. Ask one student to be the recorder for the class and have her/him write down all the suggestions that the class comes up with. The list should include at least the following items:

   plastic containers of all sizes

   steel cans (School cafeterias have #10 cans; they're nice and large for deeper sounding instruments.)

   plastic bottles

   egg cartons

   sticks of all sorts and sizes

   scrap paper

   fabric scraps

   plastic meat trays

4. Ask the students to bring in as many of the listed things as possible (see Recycled Needs Chart). **Remind them that if they are bringing in an item that once held food or a beverage, to rinse it out thoroughly!** If by some chance you do have a child who brings in unrinsed items, have the child rinse the item in the school bathroom or the janitor's closet. Also, remind the students that they should ask permission before taking anything from home.

NOTE: Discourage students from bringing in glass bottles. They also need to make sure that the cans they bring in don't have sharp edges. Check all items as they arrive to insure that they are safe.

5. On the day you decide to actually make the instruments, make sure you have an ample supply of masking tape, clear tape, glue, string, staplers, scissors, nuts and bolts, rubber bands and whatever else you feel might be useful.

6. Some things that aren't recycled items that might make a great addition to the supplies are: soda straws, plastic forks, knives, spoons, unpopped popcorn, uncooked rice, bird seed, marbles, dried beans, pebbles, sand, and whatever.

7. Ask the kids to name as many instruments as they can. As they name different instruments, ask how each makes sound. Is it vibrating strings? Columns of air that vibrate? Tightly stretched skins that move quickly back and forth?

8. After enough instruments have been named, ask what seems to be the word that keeps popping up when discussing what makes an instrument's sound? Yes, *vibrating*! So how are they going to make their instruments vibrate?

9. Be *sure* to remind the students that they are out to create *new* instruments, not just copy already created ones. Ask them to think of a pleasing sound, and then try to create an instrument that recreates that sound. They should also try to make an instrument that can change its sound. (That way the band might not end up being totally composed of percussion instruments.)

10. Allow the students to work on their instruments for at least a half hour. The teacher should circulate and encourage the students, act as a listener, but try not to give advice or "how to make it better" advice.

    If a student finishes his/her instrument before the other students, you might suggest that he/she assists another student who could use some help.

11. When the instruments are completed, ask the students to try to play them. Naturally, there will be great cacophony. When the noise quiets, ask what can be done to improve the band.

12. Allow the students to come up with a fair plan that allows each student to make their own sounds which are hopefully in harmony with other students' instruments.

13. When it looks like a break is needed, ask the students to each show their instruments and explain how it works. (If you try to have individuals explain the instruments first and then play as a group, the explanations will constantly be interrupted by kids who simply can't wait to play their newly-created instruments. Why not avoid sounding like a nag, by letting them play first, share second?)

14. After the students help to clean up, you need to decide what to do with the instruments. Will you save them in a large box for another day? Should they be displayed for others to see? Should new and improved designs be attempted? Should they be taken home? Perhaps the students have a different suggestion. (Play for the principal, the PTA, the parents at "Back to School Night?"

■■■■■ RUBE GOLDBERG DEVICES ■■■■■

INTRODUCTION

Rube Goldberg was a cartoonist who delighted audiences with complex diagrams that accomplished simple tasks. This activity, which can lead up to The Recycled Invention Convention or The Seven Task Project, allows the students to create complex diagrams that don't really have to work. It just has to appear logical enough that it would work if it were actually constructed. If you ask the class to actually *create* the devices, be prepared to spend a great deal of time working out problems. It is tough to make them work!

OVERVIEW

A fun way to introduce students to problem solving is to have them create silly, fun diagrams of structures that perform a simple task through a complex series of actions.

PROCEDURE

1. Either create a Rube Goldberg device, or find a picture or drawing of one.
2. Discuss the way that the device works with the class.
3. Develop a list of simple tasks for which the class might devise Rube Goldberg diagrams. You might wish to include such tasks as:

turn on a lamp	make toast
pull the plug from a bathtub	close a drape
open a can of dog food	bait a fishhook
close an umbrella	turn on a stove
walk a dog	quiet a noisy baby
open a door	make a rocking chair rock
iron a shirt	sharpen a knife

4. Ask the students to make sketches of Rube Goldberg devices on scrap paper. As you circulate among the students, discuss how the devices might work. Try to have the students draw contraptions that might realistically work! Once the students are satisfied with a good sketch, ask them to draw it on good paper.

5. Encourage students to be creative, and provide guidance for those who are having difficulty. Be careful not to tell them how to solve the various problems that they encounter; you should ask questions that will provide the avenue for the students to solve the tasks.

6. When all of the diagrams have been completed, have each member of the class share his/her invention with the rest of the group.

RECYCLED INVENTION CONVENTION

INTRODUCTION

Problem solving for real life annoyances is the focus of this hands-on activity. Students first identify a problem, and then attempt to create a solution. One student was worried about his father, who jogged at night. So he created a jogger's vest that had battery operated lights all over it!

OVERVIEW

Students participate in a series of warm up activities and then are asked to create an invention from recycled materials. They may work on the invention in class as well as at home. This is a good activity for Back to School Night as the parents can see creative inventions that their children have made.

PROCEDURE

1. Begin by making sure that you have a "Recycled Needs Board" or some other means of students working together to obtain needed recycled materials. As a means of preparing the class for what is about to happen, you can do the Rube Goldberg lesson.

2. Next, have the class brainstorm things that "bug" them. The list of the things they find annoying will grow and grow as the ideas begin to flow. Don't worry if after an initial flurry there is silence…they are thinking. After the silence, there will be more and more ideas.

3. Ask the class if they can think of inventions that were made to meet a need in the past. For example, the safety pin was probably invented because straight pins can jab people. The alarm clock was invented so people didn't oversleep, etc.

4. After many of the already invented inventions have been discussed, ask the class to look at the annoyances that are listed on the board. What new invention would take care of one of those things? Allow discussion to continue so that the students get some ideas for how to solve some of the listed problems.

5. Review scientific method with the class and have the students sketch solutions on scrap paper.

6. Circulate around the class to make sure that students who need assistance are encouraged. Don't make suggestions, just ask good questions.

7. Announce that the contest is on. The class needs to create an invention that is a solution to a problem. The students need to construct their invention from recycled materials. Money can only be used to purchase materials such as batteries or other things that can't be found through the "recycled board" advertising. Hand out the Recycled Invention Convention Rules Sheet.

RECYCLED INVENTION CONVENTION RULES

CONGRATULATIONS

You are about to participate in the new and innovative
RECYCLED INVENTION CONVENTION!

All you need to do is create a solution to one thing that you find an annoyance.

The rules are:
Whenever possible, you should use recycled materials.
Your invention should be one that has not been invented yet.
When you present your invention, you must have a card that explains:

THE PURPOSE OF THE INVENTION

HOW IT WORKS

WHAT MATERIALS WERE USED TO MAKE IT

You also need to have a diagram of the invention.
Each invention must have your name and number on it.
Your parents may assist you, but most of the work must be your own.

The inventions are due on: _____

GOOD LUCK AND GOOD INVENTING!

Name_____   Date_____

RECYCLED INVENTION PLANNING SHEET

Please list three things that annoy you:

_____

_____

_____

What could you create to prevent these annoyances?

_____

_____

_____

Please select one idea, and sketch it here:

What would you call this creation?

_____

What materials would you need to actually create it?

_____

_____

_____

_____

Where would you obtain these materials? _____

_____

_____

8. Each invention needs to have a written explanation with it. If possible, a diagram should be made to show how it works. The invention also needs to have a name. You can have students fill out the Recycled Invention Planning Sheet to help them get started.

9. Allow class time for the class to work on their inventions. Provide paper for the explanations and diagrams. Students who work on their projects at home should provide progress reports to insure that they are indeed working.

10. On the day that the projects are to be presented to the class, each student must explain how his/her invention works, the problem it is meant to take care of, how it was constructed, and any other details that are important.

11. After all inventions have been explained, give each invention a number that must be displayed with the invention. Give each student a ballot and allow the class to circulate among the inventions.

12. Each student votes for the one that they feel is the best one. The ballot is placed inside of a sealed box.

13. The next day, the top ten vote getters are placed on display in the library.

14. All students are declared "the winners." Everyone receives a certificate, and should be heartily congratulated for producing a real invention!

section VI
WHAT ELSE?

▬▬▬▬▬▬▬ SNOW FOOLIN... ▬▬▬▬▬▬▬

INTRODUCTION

When the snow starts to fall, the kids usually are abuzz. They want to *see* the snow! So, they stand up, and in any other way possible look out the window. They focus their attention outside. Why not capitalize on the interest in the falling snow? Have the kids put on their coats and go outside!

OVERVIEW

Using hand lenses, the students try to categorize the types of snow crystals that are falling. This activity only takes about 15 minutes, but should be continued throughout the winter so that the students have the opportunity to observe different types of snow crystals.

PROCEDURE

1. Gather the following materials and go outdoors.

     hand lenses (one for each student is best)

     dark cloth. (A good size for the cloth is 12 inches by 12 inches. If no cloth is available, black construction paper will do.)

     guide to snow crystals (Have these duplicated in advance, and stored in your file cabinet, waiting for this moment!)

2. Make sure all students are properly dressed to go outdoors. Hats and gloves are a must if the temperature is below 25 degrees. Usually the school nurse or the lost and found box can assist students who are not prepared to go outdoors.

3. Give each student a hand lens and a piece of dark-colored cloth. If you don't have the dark cloth, don't worry about it. Coat sleeves work real well, too!

4. Distribute the *Field Guide to Snow Crystals* sheet to the students and discuss the types of snow crystals that are listed.

5. Ask the students to think about reasons why different types of snow crystals exist. Tell them that the different theories they come up with will be tested to see which is the most accurate.

6. Allow the students to go outdoors. Set the boundaries for them before going outside. You might need to remind them that they are still studying science, and it has not become recess or gym class.

7. Allow the students about 10 or 15 minutes to observe the snow crystals.

     —If the weather is calm and the students can find sheltered spots, ask them to sketch the snow crystals that they see.

Field Guide to Snow Crystals

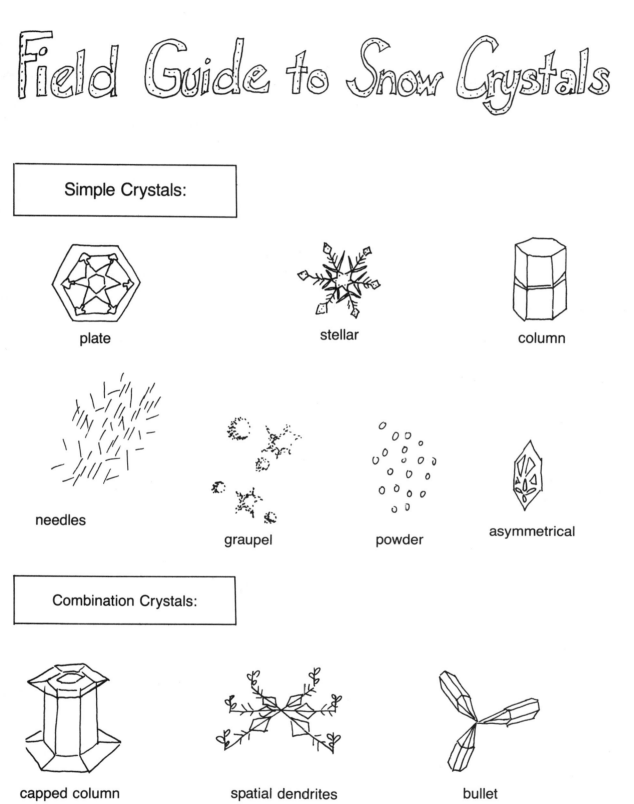

Simple Crystals:

plate

stellar

column

needles

graupel

powder

asymmetrical

Combination Crystals:

capped column

spatial dendrites

bullet

—If the weather is very cold or the wind is blowing hard, stay outdoors for only a few minutes. As students observe the crystals, circulate and discuss their findings.

8. After you return indoors, discuss the types of crystals that were found. Discuss the theories that the students have about why the different crystals are formed.

9. Develop a plan by which the class can test those theories. A good idea is to keep a classroom chart with the measurement of different factors which might determine the different types of snow crystals.

10. In reality, the factors which determine the formation of snow crystals are the conditions found in the sky where the snow crystals are formed. It is possible, after much discussion and measurement of temperature, wind speed, humidity and other weather facets, for the students to look to the place where the crystals are formed, not where they fall.

Some great books that are good for this activity are:

Stokes, Donald W. *A Guide to Nature in Winter*. Boston: Little, Brown and Company, 1976.

> This field guide not only describes snow crystals, it also includes animal tracks and habits, winter birds, winter tree identification, winter plant guide, winter insects, and galls. The book is a treasure for anyone who ventures outdoors with children in winter.

Bentley, W.A., and Humphreys, W.J. *Snow Crystals*. New York: Dover Publications, 1962.

> "Snowflake" Bentley loved the snow crystals, and spent half a century photographing them. This book is filled with the best of his remarkable photographs. Students can see the intricacies of the crystals without the need to worry that they will melt. The Dover Press reprint is an unabridged reprint of the 1931 edition of this book.

The *New York Times* printed a great article on snow crystals in the "Science Times" section on January 6, 1987. The article is worth going to the library and looking up in microfiche.

NATURAL HISTORY BOOK

INTRODUCTION

Use what you have to make the class aware of their surroundings! Have the class survey the grounds to determine what lives nearby. The rich histories of the things that share our world are reported to the class and then the written results are bound into a book for the future classes of the school.

OVERVIEW

Many different types of plants, animals and insects live near and inside the school. Why not take advantage of the local wildlife and have the students survey what lives nearby, and after completing the research on the creature or plant, write its natural history?

PROCEDURE

1. Divide the class into survey teams. Ask each team to name as many things as possible that live near the school. Students may only list the things that they actually observe. Plants, birds, insects, mammals and reptiles are all possibilities. If students find evidence of an animal, (scat, prints, feathers, claw marks, whatever!) that animal may be included.

One class created the following list:

lady bug	violet	gray squirrel
damsel fly	mullein	killdeer
leaf cutter bee	day lily	chipmunk
monarch butterfly	black raspberry	red tailed hawk
luna moth	staghorn sumac	turkey vulture
dragonfly	purple loosestrife	robin
spit bug	bergamot	chickadee
ants	dandelion	groundhog
spider	poison ivy	rabbit
housefly	goldenrod	mole

2. Discuss the teams' findings. Make a list of all the things that the class discovers on the board.

3. Ask each student to select one of the animals or plants that is listed on the board. Once an animal or plant is chosen, its name should be erased from the board.

4. When each student has a creature or plant to research, they should try to discover its habits, lifestyle, foods, enemies, unusual traits, home, etc. The student should also make a drawing of their creature or plant.

A SAMPLE NATURAL HISTORY REPORT

The sandy soil outside of the window of our classroom was acting very strangely. Grains of dirt and sand were popping from the bottom of a small, two inch hole! Who ever heard of a hole digging itself? I decided to sit down and watch this amazing hole.

After a few minutes of observation, the hole stopped digging itself. A passing ant tumbled into the steep-sided hole.

When the ant reached the bottom, a brown insect jumped out from under the soil, and threw dirt on top of the ant, burying it completely. The insect was an ant lion! And, it had just found dinner.

The ant lion, sometimes called a doodlebug, is actually the larval stage of a winged insect that looks somewhat like a small dragonfly. The larva has very powerful jaws that are used for capturing the insects that have the misfortune to fall into its sandy trap. The jaws are equipped with a poison to kill the ant lion's prey as well as a little channel by which the juices are sucked from the victim.

When the ant lion matures, it constructs a silk cocoon. Inside the cocoon, the ant lion changes from a larva to an adult. The adult will find a mate and then females lay their eggs on the sandy ground, and the cycle begins again. When the eggs hatch into larva, they dig holes in the ground and await unwary crawling insects.

The ant lion does have some predators of its own, though. One parasitic wasp flies to sandy places and carefully looks for depressions in the sand, a sign of the ant lion. When the wasp finds one, it devours it.

Ant lions are found all over North America, and I'm glad that one lives under the window of our classroom!

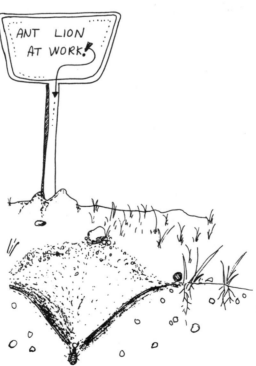

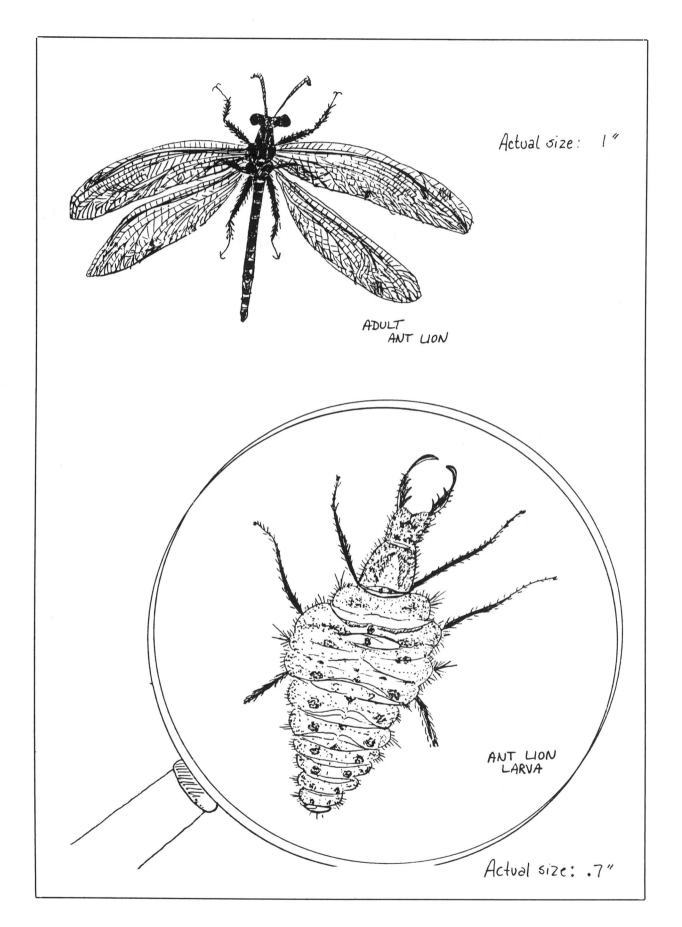

Actual size: 1″

ADULT
ANT LION

ANT LION
LARVA

Actual size: .7″

5. Each student should prepare a written and an oral report. The written reports can be collected and bound together with a cover. The book might be donated to the school library or placed in the classroom library. Encourage the students to use a lively, interesting style that will pique the curiosity of the reader. See the sample Natural History Report.

■ SCIENCE BOARD GAMES ■

INTRODUCTION

Looking for a creative, high-interest way to review with your class? Why not have the students devise their own science board games! Creating the games involves review of already covered material, as well as synthesizing that information to make it fit into the format of the game. Students develop organizational skills, communication skills, and problem solving skills as they create their games.

OVERVIEW

Students create board games as a review activity. The games are developed from recycled materials.

PROCEDURE

1. As an introduction to the project, discuss already existing board games. Ask the students to categorize those games as to how each game is won. In some games, participants need to be the first one to successfully negotiate a maze, or collect a number of items; in others the winner needs to decipher words; still others require that players apply strategies.
2. Discuss the ways in which the class can make games so that they are educational.
3. Give each student an instruction sheet and discuss the rules that are a part of this project.
4. Since one of the rules is that all games must be created from recycled materials, the class needs to discuss sources for suitable materials. Hand out *Rules of the Game*.

   —"Boards" may come from cardboard packing boxes, old pizza boxes, plywood scraps, tag board that has already been used on one side or any other material that has already been used at least once.

   —Paper needed for such things as question cards, "play" money, or whatever, should come from the classroom scrap paper pile. Save old dittos, announcements, extra letters to parents, and other paper that has only been used on one side for the scrap paper pile. Supermarket bags, and newspaper can also be pressed into service if need be.

Name_____ Date_____

RULES OF THE GAME

Your board game must:

1. Be original. You may change an already existing game, but you may not copy one.

2. Involve science concepts and be educational. You may review material from class notes, from your text, or from both.

3. Be constructed from recycled materials only. You may not spend any money on this project.

4. You must create your own game pieces and methods of moving around the board. Be resourceful. Create something new!

5. You must have written rules that everyone can understand. You may not create a game so complicated or private that no one but you can play it!

6. Although you may have help with your project, you must be the primary worker on the game. You will have to explain your game on the day it is due.

Your game is due on _____

- Game pieces can be milk container caps, soda bottle caps, hairspray can tops, cardboard cutouts or a myriad of other things. Even natural objects can fit here. Acorns, small pebbles, shells, sticks, pine cones are all okay for game pieces. The only rule with natural items is that they must be on the ground before they can be used.

- Spinners and other devices to move pieces from one place to another should be original and, preferably, creative moving devices. Brainstorm with the class to stimulate good ideas. Once, a student removed the label from a juice can. She replaced the label with a new one that had numbers written on it. To move, a player rolled the can on the floor. When the can stopped rolling, the number facing the ceiling was the number of spaces the roller could move. Others have brought in margarine tubs with numbered marbles inside. The student who was about to move simply shook the container until a marble fell out of the hole cut in the lid. That was the number of spaces to move.

5. Allow one or two class periods for the students to work on their games. Students who are stumped can get help from others who face the same project. If necessary, have the whole class make suggestions for a student who simply can't come up with an idea.

Make sure that all students have a game in mind and a plan of how to proceed before leaving the classroom.

6. On the day that the games are ready, each student explains the game that he or she has created and the rules by which that game will be played.

7. When all of the games have been explained, the students are allowed to select the games that they wish to play. Students are reminded that fair play is a must and politeness is essential. When students select games, they must play it until it is completed; no quitting mid-game is allowed.

8. The day after the "game playing days" discuss the following questions with the class. Which games:

   —were most exciting and why?

   —made you think the most?

   —were created with the greatest care?

   —did the players enjoy the most?

   —might be improved, and how could those improvements be put into effect?

   —would you grade with an A?

   —would you market it if you were a manufacturer of games?

   Some of the games resulting from this project are imaginative, complex, and fun, as well as serving as a creative review of the year's (or term's) work in science. For example, one student created a game where the playing board was an accurate map of our town. Players had to successfully answer a science question before they could move around the town.

Another game divided its board into seven parts based on the seven biomes studied in class. The players were dealt a hand of cards, each of which bore a picture of an animal, plant, climate, or characteristic of a biome. Taking turns, students placed one card at a time in the correct biome. If a player put a card in the wrong biome, he or she had to keep the card. The first student to discard all cards was the winner.

In another game, players had to travel across a maze-like board, answering the questions and earning money to fund research to save the bald eagle.

Yet another game called ESCAPE THE SPIDER'S WEB followed predator/prey relationships. In that game, one student was a spider, while the other three players were insects working together to keep out of the spider's grasp. The spider won if it caught two insects. The insects won if two successfully crossed the web from one corner of the board. The questions the players answered came from an ecology unit that stressed relationships in nature.

■■■■■■■■ A WEEK WITH A THEME ■■■■■■■■

INTRODUCTION

Politicians are always declaring that one week or another is dedicated to some cause. Why not declare your own week with a theme? Announce the theme ahead of time and have the class prepare for the week. This is a fun, active way to keep the enthusiasm level high, but, more importantly, it keeps the kids thinking.

OVERVIEW

For one week, the focus of science class is on one topic. The choice of topic is determined by the curriculum.

PROCEDURE

1. When appropriate to the science course of study, select a week that focuses on one aspect of curriculum. The focus can be almost anything (see EXTENSIONS).
2. About a month before the theme week, contact guest speakers who can come to the classroom and speak on an area of the theme.
3. Contact companies and firms who specialize in different aspects of the theme and determine whether they can donate information, speakers or other materials to enhance the study.
4. About three weeks before the theme week, have the students begin their research on specific topics that will be involved in the week. If a contest of some sort is to

be incorporated, set up the guidelines and rules and get the students started working. If the students are participating in a panel presentation, have them begin working on research for the discussion.

5. Two weeks before the theme week, notify local newspapers, radio stations, and television stations. They usually like to cover special events in the schools. Arrange for films and other visual presentations to be delivered on time.

6. One week before the theme week, have the class prepare signs, posters, and other necessary materials.

   —double check with all guest speakers and other folks involved as to the date and time that they are scheduled to do their presentation.

   —if a guest speaker can only do his/her presentation once, and there are sections of students who will miss the presentation, make arrangements to have the presentation videotaped. Make sure to secure the presenter's permission before beginning the taping process.

7. When the big week arrives, make sure to vary the types of activities. Include student panels and discussion groups. Intersperse guest speakers with films, demonstrations and other active happenings.

8. When the dust settles and the week is over, make sure that *all* of the people who helped receive a written thank you note. The guest speakers are the first ones who come to mind, as well as the corporations who donated things, but don't forget the janitors who helped set things up, the secretaries who typed letters and schedules, fielded phone calls and helped out, the cafeteria folks if they had any part in the process, the administrators, etc. The notes should be written by the students, and they should thank the person and express gratitude for the specific services that were given.

9. Make sure to have the students evaluate the week. They need to express what they liked, and what they didn't like. Ask for suggestions to make the week better, and for other speakers that might be included.

EXTENSIONS

Some of the suggestions for themed weeks are as follows:

1. "Poison Week"

Students research specific poisons that plants and animals use to gather food, protect themselves, communicate with others of their species, and whatever. The reports should focus on the poison and its use, including the type of poison, how it is manufactured, and how effective it is.

Students may present their findings in oral reports, posters, or some other display.

NOTE: Don't allow the actual poison to be brought to school, whether it is in a container, an animal or a plant. Accidents do happen!

Plants that might be researched are:

poison ivy	fool's parsley	spring larkspur
pokeweed	poison hemlock	blue flag
false helebore	bouncing bet	goat's rue
hemlock	jimsonweed	dogbane
jack-in-the-pulpit	buckthorns	atamasco-lily
skunk cabbage	Canada moonseed	butterfly weed
deadly nightshade	poison sumac	rattlebox
baneberry	Virginia creeper	wild indigo
lupine	horse chestnut	common buttercup
monkshood	American yew	fly-poison
oleander		

Animals that the students might research are:

fire ant	Portuguese man-of-war	poison dart frog
honeybee	monarch butterfly	scorpion
black widow spider	red eft	wasps
rattlesnake	brown recluse spider	gila monster
sea snake	coral snake	moray eel
jellyfish	cobra	

Guest speakers might be asked to speak on or students may wish to do research on:

Chemical poisons in the home, and safety measures to prevent poisoning.

First aid specifically focused on poisons (sun poisoning, accidental poisoning, food poisoning causes, etc.).

Successful poisonous animals. How the poison effects their prey. Why the animal isn't bothered by the poison if it eats its prey. How quickly the poison used for defense is replenished.

Poisons used throughout history, with a scientific emphasis on how they worked, and were they detectable? How were the poisons obtained? How did the people of the time deal with possible poisonings? (food tasters?) etc.

Poisons as mentioned in literature, but with a scientific focus on how the poison effected the character.

Legends and lore that accompany poisonous plants, with an emphasis on the scientific reasons for those legends and lore.

Antidote medicines and other items that should be in every home's medicine cabinet and how to use those items. As well as how the "Poison Hotline" in hospitals work.

2. Energy Week

Students can conduct home surveys of how energy efficient their homes are, or conduct a survey of the school to determine its energy efficiency. Or, they can prepare reports on the current energy use concerns. The focus does shift every ten years or so.

Have a panel discussion on which types of electricity generating plants are most effective today. The panel participants should be students. The moderator might be the school principal.

Invite utility company spokespeople to come and present the ways in which the company is trying to conserve.

Have the students prepare posters and displays of how different types of fuels are used for industries, homes and schools.

Debate wood-burning stove pollution of some other local energy issue. What should be done?

Have a contest to see who can create the best insulation package. See the GREAT ICE CUBE MELT.

3. Other Possibilities

"Ring Week" might serve as a REVIEW of topics from various areas already studied such as:

> fish scales (like trees, they add one ring per year)
>
> tree cross sections
>
> mushroom "fairy rings"
>
> gems (that are set in rings)
>
> bells (sound study)

◼◼◼ ACTIVITIES BY SUBJECT OR SKILL ◼◼◼

Review Activities

The Big Event

Science Board Games

A Week With A Theme

Student Project Activities

Awesome Critters Contest

Birds And Bird Feeders Of All Sorts

But Will It Work?

Create An Herb Garden

The Great Ice Cube Melt

Quick Kites

Really Extinct!

Recycled Invention Convention

Rube Goldberg Devices

Science Board Games

The Seven Task Project

A Towering Success

Water Clearing Devices Contest

Good Teaching Strategies

The Flow Tree

The Recycled Needs Chart

Science Question Of The Week

Seating Chart Sleuthing

A Week With A Theme

Making Your Own Equipment

Birds And Bird Feeders Of All Sorts

Create A Real Herb Garden

Kaleidoscopes Large...

...And Kaleidoscopes Small

Make the Room Into A Camera Obscura

Quick Kites

Using What You Have...Violets!

Water Equipment

Stressing Environmental Understanding

...And Kaleidoscopes Small

Awesome Critters

Birds And Bird Feeders Of All Sorts

Earthworms

Food Webs

Giant Spider Web Weaving

Incredible Insect Exhibit

Natural History Book

Nature Recycles Too!

Really Extinct!

Snow Foolin'

Spider Visits the Classroom

Tree Simulation

Water Quality Survey

Wildflower Mysteries

Focus on Scientific Method

Birds And Bird Feeders Of All Sorts

But Will It Work?

Great Ice Cube Melt

Kaleidoscopes Large...

Seating Chart Sleuthing

The Seven Task Project

Spider Counting

Testing Theories

Tomato Skins

Using What You Have...Violets
Water Quality Survey
Which Surfaces Do Earthworms Prefer?
Words, Words, Words...
Water Clearing Devices

Research Activities

Awesome Critters
Birds And Bird Feeders Of All Sorts
Create A Real Herb Garden
The Food Web Game
Natural History Stories
Really Extinct
September Time Capsule
The Spider Convention
A Week With A Theme
Window On a Decomposing Leaf

Problem Solving

Birds And Bird Feeders Of All Sorts
The Great Ice Cube Melt
Herb Garden Patterns
Make The Room Into A Camera Obscura
Recycled Invention Convention
Science Board Games
Science Question Of The Week
Seating Chart Sleuthing
The Seven Task Project
September Sleuthing
Testing Theories
A Towering Success
Tracking People In The Snow
Water Clearing Devices
Water Quality Survey
Wildflower Mysteries

Observation Skills

But Will It Work?

Earthworms

Herb Garden Patterns

Leaves to Help Seeds Grow

Science Question Of The Week

Seating Chart Sleuthing

Snow Foolin'

Spider Counting

Spider Visits the Classroom

Testing Theories

Tomato Skins

Tracking People In The Snow

Water Quality Survey

Words, Words, Words...

Wildflower Mysteries

Window On a Decomposing Leaf